er 1989
Duke of York
nnon and 23
e Southampton
Whitbread Round
Race.

Cape

t leg
ole race
re.

Leg 2
Demolition derby continues
as *Rothmans, Martela, Fazisi,
NCB* and *Maiden* break
booms.

**LEG 2
7,650 Miles**

r 1989
ch is swept
m *Fortuna*, and
near-freezing
inutes – very
here are five
d incidents in
g.

3 December 1989
All-woman crew on *Maiden*
win Class D: a great effort
by the girls in the Southern
Ocean.

FREMANTLE
Western Australia

17 November 1989
Fortuna sets new official
noon-to-noon record run of
393.8 miles, with an
unofficial 24-hour run of 405
miles recorded also. *Fortuna*
is the fastest boat in the fleet
when heavy-air running.

26 November 1989
Steinlager 2 wins close finish
after 7650 miles. *Rothmans*
and *Merit* finish only 28
seconds apart. *F & P* is
fourth after leading for most
of the leg.

**LEG 3
3,434 Miles**

2 January 1990
French yacht *Charles
Jourdan* hits a whale, badly
damaging the side of her
hull; able to patch it and
continue on to Auckland.

3 January 1990
UBF loses her mast; able to
jury rig to Auckland. *NCB*
breaks her boom again.

4 January 1990
Steinlager 2 and *F & P*
match-race to be the first
Kiwi yacht into home port,
Auckland. *Steinlager 2* wins
by six minutes in a close-
fought duel watched live on
TV in New Zealand.

4 February 1990
Re-start with the fourth leg.
The Card is converted to a
sloop after losing her mizzen
mast in a collision with a
spectator yacht.

**AUCKLAND
New
Zealand**

8 February 1990
Rucanor Sport collides with a
whale and returns to
Wellington for repairs to her
rudder. *NCB Ireland* breaks
her boom yet again.

BIG RED

GLEN SOWRY

Glen Sowry's passion for yachting began on Paremata Harbour in Wellington, where he made his mark as a young, up-and-coming yachtsman. He moved into the Olympic 470 class and competed with distinction in three World Championships, the 1987 pre-Olympic regatta in Korea and numerous European events.

His enthusiasm for offshore racing was sparked back in 1984, when he applied for a berth on Peter Blake's *Lion New Zealand* for the 1985/86 Whitbread race. It was during this race that Sowry established himself as a top-class helmsman and sail trimmer — a testament to his 470 sailing background.

Throughout the *Steinlager 2* and *Lion New Zealand* Whitbread campaigns, Sowry showed a flair for writing as he covered the race for *New Zealand Yachting, Japan Yachting* and *Yachting World* (UK) magazines. He also wrote a weekly column for the *NZ Sunday Times* during the 1985/86 Whitbread.

MIKE QUILTER

Mike Quilter graduated from Auckland University with a BSc degree, a qualification he was never to utilise as his interest in yachting drew him into a career as a sailmaker and ultimately a professional yachtsman. He has raced in most of the world's blue-water classics over the last ten years, but it was as a sailmaker for Alan Bond's victorious *Australia II* campaign in 1983 that he gained widespread recognition.

The 1985/86 Whitbread race beckoned and Quilter joined Blake's *Lion New Zealand* crew as a watch captain, alongside Grant Dalton. It was the 1987 America's Cup on board *KZ-7* in Perth that established him as a world-class navigator. Quilter became Blake's right-hand man in the Steinlager Challenge and he was responsible for the development of Big Red's computer systems.

He lives with his wife Robi, also a keen sailor, in Auckland.

Adventure means risking something;
And it is only when we are doing that
That we know really what a splendid thing life is
And how splendidly it can be lived . . .

The man who never dares never does;
The man who never risks never wins.
It is far better to venture and fail than
To lie on a hearthrug like a sleeping purring cat.

Only fools laugh at failure;
Wise men laugh at the lazy and too-contented
And at those who are so timid that they dare undertake nothing.

Alain Gerbault

BIG RED

THE ROUND THE WORLD RACE
ON BOARD STEINLAGER 2

GLEN SOWRY
MIKE QUILTER

Hodder & Stoughton
AUCKLAND LONDON SYDNEY TORONTO

To Robi and Anna

This book is respectfully dedicated to Six Four, BC, Rose, Grim, Spike, Shoebie, Jaws, Baz, Goddy, Billy, Trae, Clutch and Deano, with whom we had the privilege of sailing around the world. You wouldn't find a better bunch of guys.

Foxy and Lowlife
July 1990

Book design and typesetting by Acorn Graphics Ltd, Auckland.
Printed and bound by Kyodo Printing Co. Ltd, Singapore for Hodder and Stoughton Ltd, View Road, Glenfield, Auckland, New Zealand.

Contents

Acknowledgements

This book is the crew's story and there are certain people we wish to thank for their help in the production of this book.

First and foremost, we wish to thank Douglas Myers of Lion Nathan, without whose support and belief in Peter Blake, the Steinlager Challenge and consquently this book would never have happened.

David Bridgman, Murray Taylor and Maria Ryan of Creative Planners were a continual source of help and advice. Alan Sefton and Bruce Scott of *New Zealand Yachting* magazine and David Glen of *Yachting World* magazine (UK) allowed us to adapt material written by Glen Sowry for their magazines. John Lusk of Russell, McVeagh, McKenzie, Bartleet and Co. gave valuable legal advice. Tom Beran of Hodder & Stoughton provided enthusiasm, belief in us and helpful advice. Patrick Burke of Design Link did the artwork used on the inside cover of this book, and David Bloom and his Commercial Photographers team were a great source of photos. Russ McLean and Alan Kitto of CED Distributors (Apple Computers) kindly loaned an Apple Macintosh computer for the production of the typescript.

Lastly, but by no means least, a big thank you to Robi Quilter, for toiling long and hard on the keyboard typing out our often barely readable text and for her constructive criticism.

We are grateful to the photographers whose work is represented in this book, and acknowledge the assistance of the following photographic sources:

Steinlager 2 crew: pages 1 (right), 22, 27, 33, 34, 35, 36, 65, 72, 76, 77, 79, 80, 81, 83, 84-5, 86, 87, 90, 93, 96, 97, 98, 99, 101, 102-3, 105, 106, 107, 108, 114, 115, 116, 118, 119, 120, 122, 139, 140, 141, 145, 146, 147, 153, 154, 155, 159, 160, 161, 162-3, 165, 166, 168, 174, 175, 176, 177, 179, 180, 182, 193

Commercial Photographers: pages 8, 15, 17, 18, 19, 20, 25, 26, 28, 29, 30, 32, 38, 40, 45, 46, 49, 51, 52, 55, 56, 110, 150, 157, 158, 190

Creative Planners Ltd: pages 21, 23, 24, 37, 47, 89, 112, 127, 128-9, 131, 134, 186-7, 189, 192 (right), 195

New Zealand Yachting magazine: pages 2-3, 10, 11, 13 (right), 58, 61, 62-3, 64, 66-7, 68, 69, 71, 74, 132, 136

Fisher & Paykel Ltd: pages 13 (left), 59, 60, 92, 113

Pickthall Picture Library: pages 95, 135, 138, 142-3, 149, 167, 170

Rick Tomlinson: pages 1 (left), 50, 184, 192 (left)

Betty Rae: pages 109, 130, 185

Philip Macalister: pages 42, 43

Fotopacific: pages 124-5, 126

RNZAF: page 121

Robi Quilter: page 152

Anna Macindoe: page 31

Foreword

The Whitbread Round the World Race was first run in 1973. In those days it was an amazing adventure that involved racing through waters and across oceans unknown and uncrossed by most yachtsmen. The only information on the whims and might of the Southern Ocean came from the great days of sail: from more than 150 years ago when the immigrant ships brought the first of my ancestors to New Zealand.

The race has now gone beyond the 'adventure only' stage, to become one of the most testing yacht races of all time. The emphasis is now on going fast 24 hours a day and getting there first. This means having a no-compromise approach from the moment that the sponsor says 'yes'. For *Steinlager 2* the race was underway more than 21 months before the start gun in England.

To the crew — my very special thanks to a talented group of young New Zealanders. As well as being expert yachtsmen, you left a great feeling about New Zealand wherever you went. As ambassadors for your country you were superb.

But the grand slam win really had its beginnings many years ago. It involved all the New Zealanders who helped sponsor *Ceramco New Zealand*, *Lion New Zealand* and that amazing trimaran *Steinlager 1*. It involved the enthusiasm of every person who helped us, by believing in what we were trying to achieve. And it involved some very close and special friends and family members who stood behind us all the way.

To New Zealand, thanks for making it all possible.

Peter Blake
August 1990

CHAPTER ONE

A Star Is Born

It was during the 1985/86 Whitbread Round the World Race aboard *Lion New Zealand* that the crew formed an institution called ' the Whitbread Lifeline'. This was a pact amongst the crew that, if anybody felt tempted to do the next Whitbread in four years' time, he could immediately ring up his mates and they would dissuade him, with tales of cold, wet, windy nights in the Southern Ocean as opposed to hot showers and clean sheets at home. What weak creatures we are; one phone call from Peter Blake was all that was needed to throw that out the window. Peter had organised the finance for a couple of projects, the second being a new maxi boat for the 1989/90 Whitbread race, and that caused much excitement in the camp at Fremantle, Australia, where eight of his *Lion New Zealand* crew were competing in the America's Cup.

They had arrived in Fremantle direct from the finish of the 1985/86 Whitbread race and, although they didn't find out until later on, had apparently injected some much-needed enthusiasm, drive and discipline into the America's Cup camp. These are essential attributes for any Whitbread sailor, and were sorely needed in Fremantle. Eventually four of them made the cut, and sailed on *KZ-7* in the challenger trials. The amount they learned about sailing that year was astronomical, and all this hard-won knowledge was destined to flow directly into the new boat. Michael Fay and his campaign lifted New Zealand yachting to new heights in sailing and organisational skills, and *Steinlager 2* was to be the beneficiary.

The first project Blakey had lined up was a race around Australia. This was the Goodman Fielder Wattie Bicentennial Two-Handed Round Australia Yacht Race, a race that has the distinction of having perhaps the longest title in the history of yachting. To compete in this race Peter proposed building a futuristic 60-foot trimaran complete with a huge wing mast, a fairly radical concept for New Zealand, but then Blakey had always been a bit ahead of his time. This yacht, designed by Englishman David Alan-Williams and called *Steinlager 1*, was very successful, achieving all that was asked of her, and became the primary test-bed for many of the materials, techniques and electronics which were to play such a large part in the Whitbread yacht, *Steinlager 2*.

Steinlager 1 was built in Mairangi Bay, Auckland, by Tim Gurr and his team at Southern Pacific Boatyard, using materials and techniques new to boat-building in New Zealand. The yacht was made entirely from carbon fibre, a black synthetic material provided by SP Systems, a firm based in Cowes, England. They mixed the carbon fibre and the resin in exactly the right proportions, froze it, and then flew it out to New Zealand, where Tim and his team laid it up over wooden moulds in the shape of the boat and literally baked the whole thing in a huge oven. This resulted in a yacht that was extremely light and strong, the two most important attributes a racing yacht needs. This method of construction is also very expensive as the carbon

Steinlager 2 under construction. The boat-builders begin to lay up the carbon fibre on the mould.

fibre pre-impregnated with resin is the best product available.

The original intention was to transport the trimaran to the water using a heavy-lift helicopter; however, just before *Steinlager 1* was due to come out of the shed the helicopter company went bust. The only option was to truck her through the streets of Auckland, and this posed a few problems as there are not many streets wide enough to allow passage to a 52-foot-wide trimaran. However, where there's a will there's a relative, as they say, so the lads set off with tape measures in all directions and finally found the route of least resistance. This route involved removing only seven lamp-posts, one bus shelter, three road signs, two large trees, numerous branches and a large section of earthen bank before lifting the tri over the top of a row of high trees onto a barge in Lucas Creek at the head of Auckland's Waitemata Harbour. The Ministry of Transport and the Power Board didn't even blink at the suggested changes to Auckland's road layout, and were most helpful and courteous. There followed a memorable night's work shifting the trimaran down this route during a huge thunderstorm complete with torrential rain and continuous thunder and lightning. The lads weren't too unhappy about the atrocious weather as it helped cover the sound of chainsaws as the occasional tree in granny's front garden was trimmed back. The climax of the move was transferring the tri from one crane to another while

Lion New Zealand, *on which many of Big Red's crew served their apprenticeship.*

suspended 30 metres up in the air to get her over the trees on the edge of Lucas Creek. Those Carlton Crane boys really know their stuff.

While Peter and Mike were whizzing all over the ocean testing out this strange beast, the basis of the crew for *Steinlager 2* was forming. Kevin Shoebridge, Ross Field, Brad Butterworth, Tony Rae and Godfrey Cray all returned from various yachting contests around the world to join the team of the Steinlager Challenge, as it was called, and immediately set to work on the concepts and details of the Whitbread yacht, which was still only ideas at this stage with no definite shape or form. Blakey had commissioned Bruce Farr to design the new yacht, and wanted to provide Bruce with as much information as possible, so that he knew exactly what the requirements were when it came to putting pen to paper.

Brad Butterworth conceived and organised the sail development programme which was to play such a large role in *Steinlager 2*'s later success. Kevin Shoebridge and Tony Rae concentrated on the deck layout and interior design while Godfrey Cray, an electrician by trade, dreamed up the whole electrical system. Ross Field became a rigger and started sorting out the miles of rope and wire that would be needed.

It is to Blakey's everlasting credit that he didn't try and do all this himself, but hired the right guys early on, and then gave them a pretty free rein to look after all the details, while he concentrated on getting the basics right. This was the crux of the matter. If one could get the basics right, i.e. the design of the yacht and rig, the people and the money, the rest would follow naturally. These months had very little physical reward for all the work done other than a handful of drawings, but it was

Our fearless leader — Blakey with his son, James.

to pay huge dividends later on when *Steinlager 2* went into the water with every inch of her, every nut and bolt, every system thought and re-thought. It's a testament to this time that the yacht eventually finished the race 33,000 miles later in exactly the same configuration as when she hit the water on day one.

Armed with these collective thoughts and ideas Peter and Mike flew to Annapolis, USA, to confer with the holiest of holies, the guru of the yacht design world, Bruce Farr. Bruce, along with people like Tom Schnackenberg of America's Cup sail design fame, live on a slightly different planet from the rest of us mere mortals, who are unable to multiply seven-digit numbers in our heads. Talking to Bruce for a day, you can learn more about yachts than sailing ten times around Australia can teach you, and he is one of the main reasons for New Zealand's emergence as one of the top yachting nations in the world. However, he does charge like a wounded bull, so you've got to make every minute count.

Bruce had done the initial design work for the Whitbread yacht, the base yacht as it were, using the Wolfson tank-testing facility in Southampton. The costs of deriving this base design were met in quarter shares by syndicates headed by Peter Blake, Grant Dalton, Pierre Fehlmann (Switzerland) and Skip Novak (USA). This base design was destined to become *The Card* in the race itself. This same design was then developed further and altered to meet the particular requirements and ideas of Peter, Grant and Pierre. These boats became *Steinlager 2, Fisher and Paykel (F & P)* and *Merit,* respectively; all four yachts were different, but still variations on the same theme.

To meet their particular requirements Peter and Mike approached Bruce Farr with their ideas of what they wanted, based on the last race, which was a long, easily steered, fractionally rigged sloop. They wanted the longest yacht possible because the longer your yacht is, the faster it will go. 'There's no substitute for waterline length' as the old salts say. Also they wanted a yacht that was going to be easy to steer. By that, they meant a yacht that tracks well in a straight line and doesn't roll and broach all over the place in the big seas of the Southern Ocean, causing brave men to lose their appetites and grow ulcers the size of dinner plates. A short, heavy boat that pushes a lot of water around is terrifying in the Southern Ocean.

This Whitbread race needed a different kind of yacht to any of the previous races. This time it was a new course (prompted by the problems in South Africa), and it didn't have the long windward bashes that *Ceramco New Zealand* and *Lion New Zealand* had to endure. It was to be, if the world's weather went according to plan, a more downwind-oriented race, with a lot more spinnaker and reaching work than ever before. So with this in mind, Blakey asked Bruce Farr to investigate a ketch rig, which can set a lot more sail downwind with its two masts than a sloop can and is, therefore, faster. There hadn't been a competitive ketch for about ten years, so Peter didn't really expect to go that way, but it was his gut feeling that the option should be investigated anyway. Bruce intimated that somebody else (presumably Dalton) had asked the same questions, and the ensuing results showed that the ketch was substantially faster than the sloop around the world. So this was all pretty exciting stuff, but it was annoying that somebody else had the same information.

How does Bruce Farr decide that one design is faster than the other? Basically, he puts all the parameters of each design into a computer and comes up with what is called a velocity prediction programme (VPP). This is a computer prediction of how fast the design will sail; you can look at two VPPs and say, well yacht A is faster upwind, but yacht B is quicker downwind. But which one will sail around the world in the shortest time? To answer this you need to go a step further and sail these particular designs through the predicted weather, again on the computer.

To find out what to expect in the way of weather, the New Zealand Meteorological Service was approached, and one of their boffins, Andrew Laing, provided some excellent data based on two sources: firstly from the American Pilot charts, which describe the world's weather based on reports from shipping, built up over the last 200 years, and which have evolved into an invaluable aid to mariners; and secondly from data of several years of actual weather for the oceans and seasons the Challenge team was interested in. Armed with this predicted weather, Bruce Farr could then race various designs around the world on his computer, and it was quite fun seeing which boat would win, achieving shorter and shorter times as the designs were developed.

A design was reached that, in retrospect, looked very similar to *F & P*. Everybody seemed happy except Blakey, who, acting on another of his gut feelings, was pushing Farr to investigate the fractional rig concept. Bruce was against this as he didn't think the idea had much merit, and put it off until the very last morning in Annapolis. Only a couple of hours before Peter and Mike were due to fly home, he finally consented to run that idea through his computer, just to get Blakey off his back, and lo and

Know your enemy — Grant Dalton, skipper of the 'white shark'.
Bruce Farr — guru of the yacht design world.

behold a rocket ship emerged. All of a sudden the boat was getting longer and the masts were jumping up in height as Bruce raced to give Peter and Mike an answer before they left to catch their plane. Bruce penned the basis of *Steinlager 2* as they ran out the door, and they flew home happy in the knowledge that this design might actually be something special.

Peter and Mike felt excited about the new design, which they knew nobody else could have because everyone had already started building their boats, but they had a few problems convincing the lads back home. When they announced to the crew that they proposed to build an 84-foot ketch that weighed in at 35 tonnes, their jaws dropped in unison, and they stared at them as if they had been smoking drugs the whole time they were in Annapolis. The Challenge team was expecting a fractional sloop, a 'middle-of-the-road' boat, and reacted to the idea of a fairly extreme boat with a certain amount of horror. However, interest gathered and shock dwindled as they all pored over the projected speeds and times, and gradually everyone was won over to the idea and became infected with the same enthusiasm.

The interior concept was based on a modern round-the-buoys racer. We considered the Round the World race to be no more than just a long day-race, so we wanted a completely stripped-out racing machine, with no consideration given to comfort, and little consideration given to resale. We figured that so long as the boat won it didn't matter if the interior wasn't too palatial. Down below we tried to keep things simple, clean and functional. It was most important that everything was kept light, that the bunks were dry and comfortable, and that you could eat hot food under all conditions. So long as you could eat and sleep adequately the rest didn't matter. In an effort to keep the boat dry down below in the Southern Ocean we put as few openings in the deck as possible, and this was very successful, although it meant the boat was almost intolerably hot in the tropics because there wasn't much ventilation. However, you can't have it both ways. We considered putting a heater in for the Southern Ocean legs, but thought 'No way mate, we're Kiwis, we'll tough it out', so left it off in the interests of saving weight. We were to wonder about the wisdom of that decision later when we had icicles forming on the ends of our noses.

We had an exciting design that the whole team felt happy about, a boat that had been designed to the 'nth' degree by a bunch of guys who knew exactly what they wanted. The time had come to stop planning and start building, but we also had a trimaran to race around Australia.

While Brad and Kevin looked after the day-to-day construction details of *Steinlager 2,* the rest of the team took *Steinlager 1* across the Tasman Sea to compete in the Two-Handed Round Australia Race. This involved Peter and Mike racing the boat, with Tony, Ross and Godfrey driving around Australia in a couple of four-wheel-drive vehicles acting as the back-up shore crew. This was a very successful expedition, racing through a variety of conditions ranging from the heat and sea snakes of the Timor Sea to a fully fledged gale off Cape Leeuwin. Contact was maintained with the shore crew twice daily by radio, at which times they would delight in regaling Peter and Mike with the details of their day's travel. On one such occasion, after

Steinlager 1 *at speed.*

Peter and Mike had been at sea for over a week, the shore crew embarked on a long, slurred description of the girls they had observed sunbathing au naturel on the beach, followed by a detailed explanation of the menu that night. On *Steinlager 1* they were listening with much amusement to this alcoholic babble over the radio when they were surprised by a 30-knot squall which had sneaked up unseen while they were down below. Both Peter and Mike raced up on deck to find all hell breaking loose and, as they struggled to get things under control, Tony could still be heard on the radio rambling on about the cherry and the fresh whipped cream on his cheesecake!

Because of this race, systems and techniques were developed that were to stand us in good stead later on, as many of the electronics used on *Steinlager 1* were really developed primarily for use on *Steinlager 2*. It's one of the funny things about life that you can't just buy a whole array of electronic devices, install them on your boat, press the 'on' switch and presto you're away. It just doesn't happen like that. Invariably, it takes the thick end of a year to get everything running properly, all instruments interfaced with each other and all the computer software debugged. By the end of the *Steinlager 1* campaign everything was working well, so when the technology was transferred to *Steinlager 2* we were effectively a year ahead of our opposition in getting the electronics package up and running. Most of the instruments were installed by a boffin named Bruce Lowrie, from Crystal Electronics, whom the boys immediately nicknamed 'Big O' because of his remarkable resemblance to Roy Orbison. As soon as he walked into the yard everybody would start singing 'Pretty Woman'. We owe a lot to Big O for the success of our navigation systems.

But three days before the start of the Round Australia Race, Peter received the horrific news from Brad and Kevin that they had major delamination problems with the beloved *Steinlager 2*. It was like an atomic bomb had been dropped on the whole camp, for it looked as if the hopes and dreams of a Whitbread win had evaporated in one phone call. Peter hurried back to Auckland where he found that the whole boat was falling apart before his very eyes. A meeting was called with John Lusk, the Steinlager chairman of trustees, and Ron Endley, then managing director of New Zealand Breweries, to discuss the pros and cons of continuing the project. This meant turning around and building a whole new boat complete with new moulds as the original moulds had been broken while extracting them from the first hull. Ron Endley said, 'Let's do it', and took our case to Douglas Myers, chief executive of Lion Nathan, who to his eternal credit gave the go-ahead to build *Steinlager 2B*, as we called it. The first job was to break up the delaminated hull and deck with a chainsaw and sledge-hammers. This must have been a soul-destroying task for the boat-builders who had slaved long and hard to give us the best job possible on the first hull. *Steinlager 2A* was broken up and stored in two 20-foot containers at the back of the boatyard. The boat itself must have hated being chopped up, because it struck back in the only way it could when Wilkie, the storeman at the boatyard, opened up one of the container doors and a large piece of bow fell out, striking him on the forehead, splitting his eyelid and knocking him out cold. She had the last laugh.

Work started on the new moulds and Tim Gurr and his team came to the party once more and, along with Derek Ness of SP Systems who provided the materials, completed the new boat — from the time the 'go' button was pushed until launching — in only 17 weeks. This must be some sort of world record, as the only pieces they could salvage from the original boat were the aluminium load-bearing space frame and some interior partitioning. On the plus side of losing the first boat was the fact that the second boat turned out to be a better-finished product than the first. Human nature being what it is, the second time you build something, it's always easier as all the problems have been sorted out the first time around.

Douglas Myers, chief executive of Lion Nathan — the man behind the Challenge.

We were at pains to hide the fact that the yacht was ketch rigged. We figured we were onto a winner and didn't want the other syndicates — who obviously hadn't thought of looking at the ketch option — to realise what we were doing and perhaps have time to change their boats to a similar concept. The speed differences between the sloop and the ketch on the computer were so enormous that we thought even a cursory glance at some figures by the other syndicates would galvanise them into changing.

Finally we had a yacht ready to go in the water, and although we had to build two of them we knew we had a special boat on our hands. Some boats have it, some boats don't. It's an indefinable thing where everything feels right. Our new Whitbread entry felt good, looked good and ultimately was good.

One week before launching. The boat-builders prepare to lower Steinlager 2 onto her keel.

It's not hard to see how she earned the nickname, Big Red.

'Men At Work'.

CHAPTER TWO

The Men Behind The Man

Selecting a Whitbread crew is not just about selecting a group of good yachties. Probably the most important factor is compatibility, but many skippers seem to forget this. One of Peter Blake's greatest attributes is his ability to mould a team of people who are not only top yachtsmen, but also get on well together. When you're all going to be stuck together on a small boat for a month at a time, the last thing you need is a boat full of prima donnas.

Because of the nature of the Whitbread race, it is essential that the boat be able to remain self-sufficient while at sea. This means that you must have the knowledge and facilities on board to carry out repairs, whether they be on the sails, mast, generator or the boat's electronics. Therefore, it is essential that the crew all have expertise in these fields. Amongst the crew of *Steinlager 2* were five sailmakers, three riggers, a boat-builder, two electricians and two engineers — which meant that we were able to maintain and repair most anything on board.

These are the men Peter Blake chose in his bid to win the 1989/1990 Whitbread Round the World Race.

The Man   *Peter Blake*

Position:	SKIPPER
Nickname:	SIX FOUR (6' 4")
Age:	41
Profession:	PROFESSIONAL YACHTSMAN

What Peter hasn't done in offshore racing isn't worth knowing about. Probably the most experienced ocean racer in the world, he has sailed more than 500,000 miles, winning two Fastnet Races, two Sydney-Hobarts and numerous other races.

CHARACTERISTICS:
Known universally for his height and Viking looks. Often gets stick from the crew as to when he's going to settle down and get a haircut and a decent job. A tea drinking addict, he handles stress by consuming vast quantities of the aforementioned beverage laced with large quantities of sugar. A superstitious character as Vikings are wont to be, often resorted in calm conditions to scratching the boom and whistling in an effort to attract the breeze. Peter is a superb leader of men and was totally respected by the crew. Not averse to a bit of stirring himself, he was happy to get back what he gave.

The Men   Mike Quilter

Position:	NAVIGATOR
Nickname:	LOWLIFE
Age:	36
Profession:	PROFESSIONAL YACHTSMAN/SAILMAKER

University educated with a BSc in Zoology, not an altogether useless qualification with the crew of *Steinlager 2*'s eating habits. Lowlife is another highly experienced individual having competed in two Admiral's Cups, three Kenwood Cups and two Southern Cross Cups. Mike was a sailmaker for the winning *Australia II* team in the 1983 America's Cup. He then became a watch captain on *Lion New Zealand* in the 1985/86 Whitbread before heading to Perth to be navigator aboard *KZ-7* in the America's Cup.

CHARACTERISTICS:
A descendant of the 'Werethefarkawie' tribe, Lowlife was sometimes referred to as the 'Naviguesser'. He bore the brunt of the crew's wrath if the weather conditions being experienced on deck were not to their liking. There was much conjecture as to Lowlife's heritage when, after spending four weeks in the tropics down below in his nav station, he still had a better tan than any of the guys up in the sun. A chronic chocolate addict, he was often responsible for the cook's chocolate rations disappearing out of the pantry. To this day Mike is unable to figure out why he's called 'Lowlife'.

Brad Butterworth

Position:	WATCH CAPTAIN OF 'KIWI REDS'
Nickname:	BILLY BUNTER
Age:	31
Profession:	PROFESSIONAL YACHTSMAN/SAILMAKER

Brad trained as a sailmaker with Tom Schnackenberg at North Sails before running his own sailmaking business. Starting out as a successful dinghy sailor, Brad switched his attention to keel-boats where he quickly made his mark with a very successful Southern Cross regatta in 1985. Having competed in numerous match-racing regattas, Brad was recruited as tactician on *KZ-7* in Perth, after which he sailed on *Propaganda* in the winning Admiral's Cup team in 1987.

CHARACTERISTICS:
Like all top tacticians, Brad is incredibly devious, always in the thick of any rumours on the boat, and he had an uncanny knack of turning the heat away from himself. A connoisseur of snack food, Brad was never without a supply of biscuits, chocolate or contraband lollies on board. Occasionally had difficulty giving his watch orders when his mouth was stuffed with one of these commodities. He was never more than a couple of hours away from a TV and video in port. The low point in the Whitbread for Brad was the poor quality of Uruguayan TV.

As one of the top tacticians in the world, Brad's experience was invaluable on board and on numerous occasions, particularly finishing in Auckland, his abilities paid big dividends. Sometimes when course selection seemed complicated, Brad could simplify the issue with his clear, logical thinking.

Tony Rae

Position:	PITMAN (KIWI REDS)
Nickname:	TRAE / DR MUNGBEAN
Age:	28
Profession:	PROFESSIONAL YACHTSMAN/SAILMAKER

Trae's passion with the Whitbread began in 1981 when he applied for a position aboard Peter Blake's *Ceramco New Zealand*. With not enough experience he missed out, but by 1985 he had rectified that situation and joined *Lion New Zealand*. In addition to having sailed a Whitbread, Trae has raced in the Kenwood Cup and numerous regattas in California. He sailed as mainsail trimmer aboard *Kiwi* in the 1987 Admiral's Cup victory. Trae was also mainsail trimmer aboard *KZ-7* in the America's Cup.

CHARACTERISTICS:
Trae is almost obscenely fit. As well as being the boat's medic, he was also in charge of crew fitness. He displayed sadistic tendencies by trying to cripple the crew with early morning training. Trae's biggest disappointment of the Whitbread race was that none of the crew needed any major surgery at sea. At present he is the world record-holder for the most Weet-Bix consumed at one sitting and his life's ambition is to appear on a Weet-Bix card. Trae is an excellent trimmer, with a wonderfully dry sense of humour.

Dean Phipps

Position:	BOWMAN (KIWI REDS)
Nickname:	DEANO
Age:	25
Profession:	SAILMAKER

Deano learnt his sailmaking with North Sails in Auckland. In 1983 he was on the sailmaking team for the British *Victory* syndicate at the America's Cup. Similarly, Deano was involved in the 1987 America's Cup in Perth, this time with Alan Bond's Australian syndicate. Starting out in P Class, he moved into keel-boats, having sailed in the 1985 Admiral's Cup, Southern Cross and One Ton Cup. Deano's big success came in the 1988 One Ton Cup where he sailed as bowman on *Propaganda,* which won the regatta.

CHARACTERISTICS:
Deano, alternatively known as Kahu because of his ancestry, seemed happiest hanging up in the rig or out on the end of the spinnaker pole, where he did an excellent job. Not known for his eloquent speech, Deano was particularly difficult to understand when he was yelling excitedly from the top of the mast. He is quite possibly the world's worst tea and coffee maker. Deano is one of those happy people who walks around all day with a smile on his face.

Mark Orams

Position:	TRIMMER (KIWI REDS)
Nickname:	MARKO / CLUTCH
Age:	27
Profession:	REGIONAL PLANNER

Marko came from a very successful dinghy-racing background having won national titles in Flying Ants, 470s and Windsurfers. Relatively limited in ocean-racing experience, he more than made up for it with his helming and trimming abilities. As one of the last guys to join the project he fitted in very quickly.

CHARACTERISTICS:
Marko soon became known as Clutch Cargo because of his generous chin and was on the end of some sharp humour. Not to be outdone at a crew dinner, with a glass of 'chin and tonic' in his hand he sang his version of 'Hey Big Spender':

'The minute he walked in the joint,
you could see he had a jaw of distinction ...'

Marko established himself as the boat's poet and also a leading proponent of head-banging music. In charge of the deck gear on the boat, he was one of the hardest-working guys aboard.

Ross Field

Position: | WATCH CAPTAIN
OF 'THE DUKES OF HAZZARD'
Nickname: | ROSE
Age: | 40
Profession: | PROFESSIONAL YACHTSMAN

An ex-police detective, Ross took up full-time yachting to sail on *NZI Enterprise* in the last Whitbread. Originally from New Plymouth, he has sailed in numerous local events including racing his Young 88 *Paddy Wagon* in the double-handed Round North Island race. Ross also sailed on *Propaganda* in the 1987 Admiral's Cup.

CHARACTERISTICS:
Ross is a large man in every respect. Always on the receiving end of the crew's humour about his age, even though he is fitter and stronger than most people half his age. Not the most agile crewman around the deck, it was generally believed he had trouble manoeuvring his wheelchair around the winches and genoa tracks. Always driving when disaster strikes, whether it be a car, trimaran or maxi yacht, he will roll it, break it or broach it. Ross's greatest attribute was his drive and enthusiasm, which ensured that the boat was always being sailed at 100 per cent.

Graham Fleury

Position:	PITMAN (THE DUKES)
Nickname:	GRIM
Age:	30
Profession:	SALES REPRESENTATIVE

Graham's background as a boat-builder, combined with his rigging experience, made him a valuable crew member. Learning to sail dinghies in the Bay of Islands, he soon graduated into the Auckland keel-boat scene. Having raced in two Kenwood Cups and numerous events in America, he joined *NZI Enterprise* for the last Whitbread. Before joining Steinlager Challenge, Graham was campaigning a Soling in Europe and Australia in a bid for the 1988 Olympics.

CHARACTERISTICS:
Grim has the distinction of possibly being the world's hairiest man. The crew thought he made his movie debut starring in 'Gorillas in the Mist'; he is apt to growl and eat people when woken up from a deep sleep. Grim is a gentle giant, strong and a good all-rounder, who along with Ross and Jaws made up the boat's rigging department. This select group provided endless amusement for the rest of the crew with their incessant arguing over how to do the smallest of jobs.

Craig Watson

Position:	BOWMAN (THE DUKES)
Nickname:	SPIKE
Age:	23
Profession:	DRAUGHTSMAN

Spike, as he is universally known, came from a successful dinghy-racing background, first beginning in P Class and graduating to 470s and Lasers. Before joining the *Steinlager* crew, Spike had been racing aboard *Emotional Rescue* in the 1988 Kenwood Cup. Having trained as a mechanical draughtsman, Spike's engineering skills were to be of great value throughout the race.

CHARACTERISTICS:
A leading figure in the radical haircut and colourful clothes department, Spike was usually found off-watch plugged into his walkman, wound up to maximum volume. He was good at repairing any tricky engineering problems that nobody else wanted to know about. As one of the new boys on the block, he fitted in right away and his youthful enthusiasm kept the older members of the crew on their toes.

Glen Sowry

Position:	TRIMMER (THE DUKES)
Nickname:	FOXY
Age:	27
Profession:	ELECTRICIAN

Originally from Wellington, for which he always got a hard time, Glen moved to Auckland to pursue his yachting career. Starting out in P Class, he won national titles in Junior Cherubs, Windsurfers and 470s. Glen has also competed successfully in numerous international 470 events. Joined *Lion New Zealand* for the Whitbread, and also raced in the Southern Cross and Kenwood Cups as well as the 1988 One Ton Cup.

CHARACTERISTICS:
Throughout the race Foxy dropped enough deck gear overboard to outfit a modern One Tonner. A good helmsman, although he had to hang on tight in a fresh breeze to avoid being blown off the wheel. Along with Goddy, he was responsible for maintaining the boat's electrical system and came under constant abuse and was held personally responsible if something didn't work.

Kevin Shoebridge

Position:	WATCH CAPTAIN OF 'THREE MEN AND A BABY'
Nickname:	SHOEBIE
Age:	27
Profession:	PROFESSIONAL YACHTSMAN/SAILMAKER

Another sailmaker, Shoebie has packed more yacht racing into his 27 years than most serious racers do in their lives. Shoebie has sailed in two Admiral's Cups, including the *Propaganda* campaign, Kenwood Cup, One Ton Cup and the last Whitbread on *Lion New Zealand*. He earned a place as a trimmer aboard *KZ-7* in Perth.

CHARACTERISTICS:
Shoebie is forever getting a hard time about his height, or lack of it. His favourite song was 'I Did It My Way'. Fanatical about any unnecessary weight on board the boat, he was occasionally referred to as 'Gestapo Shoebridge'. Shoebie took his watch captain's role seriously and always drove the boat flat out. He was equally adept at driving the boys into the bar in port and naturally assumed a social director's role when ashore. A popular member of the crew, Shoebie was one of the key players.

Barry McKay

Position:	PITMAN (THREE MEN AND A BABY)
Nickname:	BAZ
Age:	22
Profession:	BOAT-BUILDER

The youngest crew member, Barry was also the only South Islander aboard, having grown up in Dunedin where he began his sailing in P Class and Starlings. He cruised and raced in the Pacific extensively including the Auckland-Suva race. Working for Tim Gurr at Southern Pacific Boatyard, Barry was involved in the building of both *Steinlager 1* and *Steinlager 2*.

CHARACTERISTICS:
Baz was the ship's philosopher. He broke almost everything he touched whether it be cutlery, bathroom walls, boathooks, hotels etc. Fortunately, he is an excellent shipwright, so he could fix everything he broke. He deserves a knighthood for his efforts in building and fitting a new mizzen chainplate at sea on the sixth leg. Although he was the youngest, Baz was also the strongest guy on board and good at everything. He had the distinction of being able to eat twice as much as anyone else, three times as fast.

Godfrey Cray

Position:	BOWMAN (THREE MEN AND A BABY)
Nickname:	GODDY
Age:	30
Profession:	ELECTRICIAN

Godfrey was jointly responsible for maintaining the boat's electrics and engine. A vastly experienced offshore racer, he is a Whitbread veteran, having been aboard Digby Taylor's *Outward Bound* in the 1981/82 Whitbread and *Lion New Zealand* in the following Whitbread. Goddy also raced in the winning Southern Cross Cup team in 1983 and sailed as bowman for Rod Davis in three Citizen Cup match-racing regattas.

CHARACTERISTICS:
Goddy has a wonderful sense of humour, the type that keeps the crew laughing by making himself the butt of many of his own jokes. Responsible for taking much of the on-board video footage, Goddy was under constant pressure from the crew to win the Golden Globe award for the best footage during the race. A multi-talented fix-it man, he was equally adept fixing things at the top of the rig or on the engine. Sailing in his third Whitbread as bowman, we held grave fears for his sanity.

Don Wright

Position:	TRIMMER (THREE MEN AND A BABY)
Nickname:	JAWS
Age:	31
Profession:	RIGGER

Jaws is a veteran of Peter Blake's *Ceramco New Zealand* crew from the 1981/82 Whitbread. Before joining *Ceramco* he raced aboard the maxi yacht *Condor* in England and the Caribbean. In 1986 he crewed aboard *Equity* in the winning Kenwood Cup team. Having run his own rigging business in Auckland for five years, Jaws could not resist the invitation to have another go at the Whitbread.

CHARACTERISTICS:
Jaws had the dubious distinction of being even shorter than Kevin Shoebridge. He discovered midway through the race that he was hard of hearing and the off-watch were constantly woken by his watch mates yelling at him. Jaws displayed amazing stamina at any after-match function, normally outlasting anyone else on the crew. Always the first to go up the rig whenever a problem occurred and, contrary to his nickname, Jaws was the slowest eater on board. He was forever meticulously checking the boat and was normally the first to discover any problems.

Cole Sheehan

Position:	COOK
Nickname:	BC
Age:	28
Profession:	CHEF

BC trained and qualified as a chef in Auckland, working in top-class restaurants before being bitten by the yachting bug and dropping everything to sail in the 1985/86 Whitbread aboard *Lion New Zealand* as cook. Since then he has crewed extensively on luxury cruising yachts in the Caribbean and Pacific.

CHARACTERISTICS:
Probably the world's most laid-back man. Beautiful women fell in love with him all over the world, but BC was normally more interested in drinking with his mates, which we could never understand. An all-round good guy and sportsman, BC was difficult to upset. He is an excellent cook who always made it look easy. It was important to keep on the right side of BC as you never knew what he was putting in the stew — he could always have the last laugh.

Martin Ford

Position:	SHORE MANAGER
Nickname:	JAAPI
Age:	42
Profession:	LAWYER

Jaapi, as he is known worldwide because of his South African heritage, is a very experienced offshore yachtsman in his own right. Having raced extensively on *Mistress Quickly* and *Condor*, he sailed as a rigger aboard *Lion New Zealand* in the last Whitbread. Jaapi did the job that many of the other syndicates had three people doing, and was responsible for the smooth running of our shore-based operation.

CHARACTERISTICS:
Jaapi became the crew's golf coach during our stay in Punta and could otherwise be found staring at his computer screen, or wheeling and dealing with local authorities. The most important part of Jaapi's job was ensuring that we had vast quantities of Steinlager, and rum and Coke, waiting for us dockside at the completion of each leg. At the beginning of the Whitbread, Jaapi had a mobile phone surgically attached to his head, where it has remained ever since.

CHAPTER THREE

Shaping The Future

It's always a nerve-racking time when launching a new yacht, waiting to see if all the numbers were calculated correctly and the yacht floats to her lines. Because of the building delay *Steinlager 2* had to be rigged and sailing as soon as possible. 'Big Red' was slipped into the water at Westhaven, far from the madding crowd, and launched privately without any fuss. This practice stems from way back when the old boat-builders used to sneak a new vessel into the water the night before the public launching to check that she floated to her lines. If not, extra ballast could be hastily added so everything would be rosy on launching day.

The first job after launching was to rig the yacht. The masts on these Whitbread yachts are so tall and sophisticated that there was only one extrusion in the world that was suitable for our yacht, one made by Sparcraft in England. However, when we approached Sparcraft intending to buy a mast from them, they advised that they had signed a contract with Grant Dalton of *F & P* selling him an exclusive extrusion. We were a bit nonplussed to say the least, and this immediately changed our attitude towards Grant's campaign. If he wanted war, so be it.

The alternative was to design and build our own extrusion but this would be very expensive. Upon further investigation we struck a deal with Pierre Fehlmann of *Merit* where we both shared the costs of a new section extruded in Switzerland. This took some delicate negotiation, and Grant's tactics turned out to be a blessing in disguise as we ended up with an excellent mast which we thought superior to the Sparcraft one. Because we were using the same section mast as Fehlmann, he was convinced that we had a fractional sloop, so this helped keep that rumour going a while longer. The Swiss extrusion was shipped out to New Zealand and assembled by Steve Wilson from Southern Spars who made an excellent job of it, making extensive use of titanium in many of the fittings in an effort to save weight aloft. A mizzen mast was ordered from Australia using a bogus name under the pretence that it was for another yacht. We even went as far as obtaining a plan from Bruce Farr of a fractional sloop, which we distributed to sail lofts and rig manufacturers for quotes. We don't know if this approach actually worked, but it was all good cloak-and-dagger stuff.

A week after launching, *Steinlager 2* was christened by Lady Myers. It was a fairly low-key affair with both *Steinlager 1* and *Steinlager 2* lined up in an impressive display of New Zealand boat-building expertise.

Unfortunately, about 15 feet of *Steinlager 1*'s port float couldn't make the party — it was drifting somewhere out in the Tasman Sea. Peter had entrusted the lads to bring the trimaran home from Sydney after the Round Australia Race. His final words were 'Don't bust it boys or we'll never be able to afford *Steinlager 2*'. You can imagine their horror when the port bow broke off exactly halfway between New

Trialling in the Hauraki Gulf.

Zealand and Australia. They had Blakey's words ringing in their ears for a week as they limped home to Auckland. Luckily, New Zealand Breweries didn't flinch; a new float was constructed and her next race was in Europe under French colours.

With *Steinlager 2* rigged and blessed, sailing trials began in earnest on Auckland's Waitemata Harbour. We had only five months before the yacht was due to be shipped to Europe, so every minute counted. We intended to start the Whitbread as we would finish it. On the first night of the race we would know exactly what speed we should be doing, which sails to have up and where they should sheet. We should be able to change spinnakers in a jiffy and have all crew work sorted out. If you have to use the first leg of the race to find out all these things then you are history. This work in Auckland was to be the basis of our sailing campaign and was an incredibly important part of our build-up to the race.

The primary ingredients needed to sort your boat out are some accurate, calibrated instruments and a computer to collect and analyse data. You can sail around the harbour saying 'This feels right' or 'That looks good' until you are blue in the face but it isn't good enough. Of course, none of the crew, with the exception of our fearless leader, had ever sailed on a ketch before so that was a whole new ball game in itself. Therefore, the early part of our sailing programme was spent trying to work out what size and shape the sails on the mizzen mast should be.

Big Red was the focus for a spectacular laser light show at her launching.

LOA	25.62 m	84 ft
BEAM	5.85 m	19.2 ft
DRAFT	3.96 m	13 ft
MAIN MAST	34.77 m	114 ft
MIZZEN MAST	25.7 m	84.3 ft
MAIN SAIL	140 m²	1512 ft²
Nº 1 GENOA	150 m²	1620 ft²
SPINNAKER	366 m²	3952 ft²
MIZZEN STAYSAIL	111 m²	1200 ft²
MIZZEN	63 m²	680 ft²

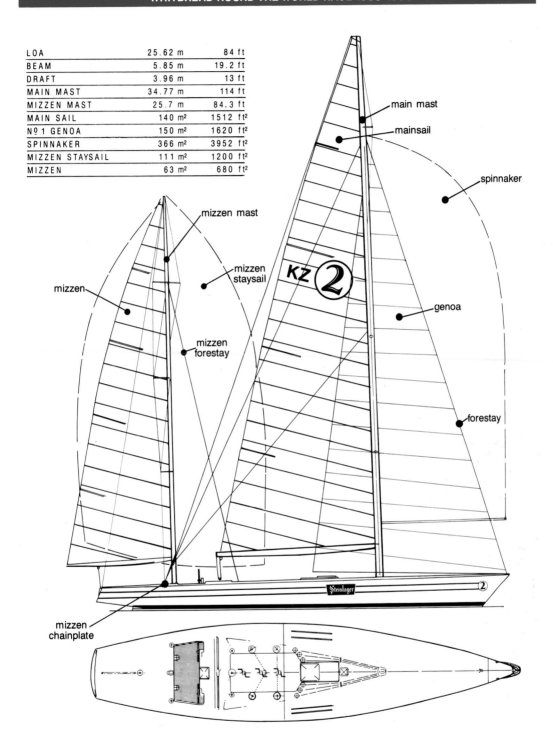

Steinlager 2 is a fractionally rigged ketch. In this fractional rig the forestay attaches to the main mast about 20 per cent of the way down from the top (as opposed to a masthead rig where the forestay attaches at the top of the main mast). The IOR rule favours this type of rig as it makes the yacht easier to handle with a spinnaker up in fresh breezes, promotes easier genoa changes because they are smaller, and the bendy mast allows more control over sail shape.

All the data from these months of sailing provided us with two major sources of information: how fast we should be sailing (target speeds) and which sails we should have up for every condition. This is vitally important because during the Whitbread race without another boat alongside you cannot gauge how well you are going. Most of the time it was just us and the horizon, so we needed some sort of targets to make sure we were sailing Big Red to her maximum at all times.

All the fastest sail combinations were recorded in our 'black book' so that even on the coldest, wettest night when your brain has switched into neutral and the temptation is to say 'She'll be right mate', you could refer to the black book and check that the right sail combination was up.

The sails were, in fact, one of the most important factors of our campaign. Without good sails we weren't going to get anywhere. Our sail-testing programme was controlled by Brad, Tony and Deano. Their priority was to quickly sort out the initial sail inventory so that North Sails could carry on and make identical replacement sails. These sails were then hoisted and checked in New Zealand before

Big Red out for her first sail on the Waitemata Harbour.

they were packed off in containers to the various ports to await the yacht's arrival. In this way we had control over every sail that was made and could leave secure in the knowledge that we would have no problems during the stopovers. We knew from past experience that the facilities for altering sails in Punta del Este were virtually nonexistent.

Dropping the mizzen staysail while sail-testing on the Waitemata Harbour.

A total of 110 sails were ordered off North Sails, which represented a colossal amount of work on their part and a sizable chunk out of our budget. They were designed by John Clinton, whom we had learned to trust in Fremantle, where he designed *KZ-7*'s sails. Under John's guidance North Sails worked 24 hours a day to produce all our sails on time and they made a fantastic job of them. Very few did we ever have to change and they played a major part in our success, particularly later on in the race when our replacement policy meant we were always up to speed while some of the other yachts were trying to eke out the mileage on their old sails.

The Steinlager Challenge was based at Princes Wharf in Auckland where we quickly developed an America's Cup-type atmosphere with the advantage of the lessons learnt in Fremantle. The day started at 7 am with a work-out at the Institute of Sport under Jim Blair's guidance. Then it was breakfast back at the office, where we discussed our priorities for the day's sailing. One hour later, having loaded sails on board, it was out onto the sparkling Hauraki Gulf for a full day's sail-testing and crew training. Back into the dock again at approximately 4 pm we would unload the sails, wash the boat down and then debrief the day's sailing.

Particular attention was paid to the clothing and wet-weather gear we were to wear in the race itself. Nobody was going to perform very well if they had buckets of icy-cold water cascading down their necks through badly designed wet-weather gear. To this end Robi Quilter spent many months collaborating with Dorlon, the manufacturers, to ensure that we had jackets and trousers that kept us dry in all conditions, and clothing that we felt comfortable with. Not only did Robi put up with all the idiosyncrasies of the crew with regard to their personal clothing, such as Blakey's trousers always being too short and Jaws's too long, but she also ran a highly successful business selling identical crew clothing that provided much-needed funds for the Challenge coffers. It was an important part of the team image that we all looked respectable on the water and in the pub afterwards.

Blakey's style of leadership appeared to be much more laid-back than Dalton's. He let the boys get on with the job and have a free run in whatever they were doing. He didn't have to order people to do things. Peer pressure from the rest of the crew made sure that nobody got out of line and that everybody pulled their weight in whatever activity was at hand, be it gym work, sailing or cleaning the boat. The gym work typified the differences that were emerging between the *Steinlager* and *Fisher and Paykel* camps. Peter picked his crew for steering and trimming attributes, size didn't matter, whereas Grant seemed to pick his crew on their physical prowess. In the middle of the night halfway through a leg you need guys who will keep trimming sails all night and not sit there and veg out, and it's not necessary to look like Arnold Schwarzenegger to do that. If you need more muscle to pull a sail down, then get more guys on deck.

Things seemed to be hotting up between the two camps, which was only natural as we were in direct competition with each other. We, on *Steinlager,* were always confident in the knowledge that we were the good guys, the men in white (bad guys are always dressed in black), and would come through and win in the end.

One of the strong suits of the ketch rig was five-sail reaching, where we were practically unbeatable.

Sailing home after a long day's sail-testing.

Such was the stress between *Steinlager* and *F & P* that we had to get Bruce Farr down to oversee the first trialling that we did together. We agreed that both boats should be in Whitbread trim for these trials, which means with all sails and water on board. There is not much to be learnt sailing in day-racing mode, so we were mightily peeved when *F & P* came out to do battle minus a few things like her spare spinnaker pole and radar in an effort to save weight. These first clashes were very tense times, finding out if we were competitive or not, especially as we had only been in the water for half the time that *F & P* had. Overall it turned out pretty even; we thought we had a slight edge, but then they probably did also.

The first time we met in earnest was over an 87-mile course round the Hauraki Gulf and after a close battle the honours went to *F & P*. It came as a bit of a shock

The Kiwis line up for the first time. Note the difference in the height of the forestays, F & P's *masthead rig vs* Steinlager 2's *fractional rig.*

to the lads that we weren't the invincible warriors we thought we were, and it showed we had a lot of work still to do, primarily on crew manoeuvres. However, we weren't too unhappy as we felt we had the basics right; it just needed a bit of fine tuning. F & P made her winning break sailing upwind in fresh air, the point of sailing which we were to find was our Achilles heel throughout the whole Whitbread race. However, our weather predictions showed that only a very small percentage of the race would be in these conditions.

The crew had naturally fallen into some sort of pattern as to where they worked around the yacht and this was formalised into watches and the various areas of responsibility defined. We were using a three-watch system: one watch on deck, one watch in their bunks and the third on stand-by, which meant they could stay below but were always ready to come on deck at a moment's notice to help the on-deck watch with a sail change. Each watch consisted of four people: watch captain, trimmer, pitman and bowman. The watch captain ran the yacht for the four hours that his watch was on deck. He was responsible for all decisions concerning sail selection and had to make sure that the boat was always sailed at 100 per cent efficiency. This was an important job as his attitude reflected how his watch performed and, consequently, how the whole boat performed during those four hours.

The pitmen and the trimmers worked in the middle of the yacht and were responsible for the setting and the trim of all the sails. They worked the halyards, set up the genoas and spinnakers for each change, and packed all the sails. In other words they did all the hard graft. They called themselves 'grunts', adopting the name the GIs gave themselves in Vietnam, although some other members of the crew thought it described the noises they made whilst trying to hold a conversation. They called their area of the boat 'adventure land' and cast scorn and derision on anybody in 'fantasy land', as they called it, down the back of the boat where the higher lifeforms existed.

The bowmen worked in 'frontier land' forward of the mast and usually were found half-buried under water or swinging up in the rig somewhere. They were the guys who always got wet, no matter what was happening, so they had to be long-suffering, fearless characters. Imagine working out at the end of the spinnaker pole in the middle of the night, and it's snowing, freezing cold and blowing a gale — the boat is tearing through the water with the bow wave rushing past inches from your feet. That sort of thing took real courage. Mind you, they had the brains of chocolate fish to be up there in the first place.

Three of the crew did not stand watches. These were our fearless leader Blakey, navigator Mike, and cook Cole Sheehan. Blakey lent a hand where he was most needed, be it on deck when the shit hit the fan, or down below in the nav station when a tricky decision was under discussion. He let everybody get on with their own job but ruled with an iron hand if things weren't going as expected. Mike swanned around in the lap of luxury down below in the navigation station, happily playing with buttons and dials while it rained or snowed outside. Cole's responsibility was

Spike going aloft to change the spinnaker halyards.

to turn out thousands of meals, sometimes under the most adverse conditions, and put up with the quirks and foibles of 14 hungry crew members. It was fortunate that he was so laid-back.

This period of trialling on the Hauraki Gulf also gave us a chance to sort out all the navigation gear. It is all well and good to have the fanciest equipment in the world on board, but it has to actually work, and provide sensible information that normal people can understand. The role of navigator in the Whitbread race has changed from the traditional role of 'Where are we?' to 'What's the weather going

Toytown on board Steinlager 2 — *the nav station.*

Deano, Baz and Trae during sail testing in New Zealand.

to do?'. We had instruments on board that could give us a position fix every one-and-a-half seconds to within 30 metres, so we knew exactly where we were all the time. The navigator's main responsibility is to try and find out what the weather is going to do in the near future, and then place the boat in the position to take best advantage of the breeze.

The single most important piece of equipment to the navigator is the weather fax. This looks very similar to an ordinary office fax and if one dials up the right radio frequency at the right time, you can receive and print out a pressure map similar to the weather map you can see in any daily newspaper. These maps are broadcast by coastal stations all over the world and one of the tricks is knowing which station gives the best maps for the area you are interested in. This is one area where Blakey's 20 years of ocean-racing experience gave us an edge.

These pressure maps could then be digitised into the Apple Macintosh computer and you could sail your yacht through that weather pattern, on the computer, and look at all possible course options, picking the one that took you closest to wherever you were going. The weather routing software that enabled us to do this was at the forefront of yachting technology. A great many hours were spent in Auckland trying the system out, locating and fixing as many bugs as possible. In keeping with the rest of the boat, we wanted all the navigation packages to be up and running correctly on the first day of the Whitbread race. The Macintosh ran 24 hours a day and not only provided us with the weather routing information, but also the performance data that kept the crew on their toes. The Macintosh performed faultlessly throughout the entire race and played a key role in making us look pretty smart on the race course.

The weather fax was the navigator's lifeblood, but he could also receive weather reports by Morse, telex and voice broadcasts. He could receive photographs of the earth's surface direct from the NOAA Satellites. All this information enabled the navigator to build up a fairly comprehensive picture of what the weather was likely to do. We had all these wonderful pieces of equipment on board, but as everyone knows, half the time the weather maps are completely wrong. Then the navigator was held personally responsible if the weather turned nasty instead of the balmy sunshine he had predicted so confidently. To help Mike interpret all this data the New Zealand Meteorological Service ran a couple of training courses in Wellington, so that at least he could sound as if he knew what he was talking about.

While Mike was getting a headache trying to sort out his 402 buttons and knobs in the nav station, Tony Rae was learning to become a medic. We had decided not to take a doctor on board, as many of the yachts in previous races had done. It was too much of a yacht race now to justify carrying someone who was picked for attributes other than sailing skills. Scott Hollingshead, a paramedic from the St John Ambulance Service in Auckland, took Trae under his wing, taking him out on the road on many evenings. It wasn't long before Trae was chasing crew members around the boat, hoping to tie them up so he could practise inserting drips and other such scary procedures that the boys didn't want to know about. Because of his semi-

Crew training during the Round New Zealand Tour.

vegetarian diet Trae was quickly christened 'Dr Mungbean'. Luckily there were very few injuries and Dr Mungbean's casebook remained a slim volume.

It was time to set off on a promotional tour around New Zealand. This gave us a chance to show the flag for New Zealand Breweries, but more importantly from the crew's point of view, it gave us a chance to sail out in the ocean and get a feel for the big red beast we had invented. Sailing in a straight line for more than a day enabled those who weren't as good on the helm as some of the others to spend extra time steering and so bring themselves up to scratch.

On the first few windy nights at sea, Big Red seemed a bit of a handful with all the sails set and only four on deck, but as the systems were sorted out it gradually became less and less of a problem. Immediately it became apparent that we had a yacht that was a lot easier to steer than the frightening *Lion New Zealand,* which was our only benchmark. *Steinlager 2* appeared to be considerably faster; so much faster, in fact, that it was hard to believe. There was also little tendency for the boat to roll whilst running downwind in heavy air, so that augured well in the ulcer department.

We experienced some pretty nasty weather whilst in Foveaux Strait and it was there that Ross's watch earned the title of 'the Dukes'. Driving the boat hard one day, they were laughing and shouting as they launched the yacht off one wave after another. Everybody else was hanging on for dear life down below, and immediate comparisons were drawn with the television programme 'The Dukes of Hazzard' and the techniques they employed to jump their car over rivers and cliffs. Thereafter, Ross's watch was always known as the Dukes.

Another significant feature of the tour was the rise and fall of a certain John Lusk. John was the chairman of trustees to the Steinlager Challenge who, along with Richard Green and Mike Smith, controlled the purse strings of our project. Blakey invited John to sail on Big Red from Wellington to Christchurch. The crew were a bit apprehensive at having one of the head honchos on board and so treated him with due respect at first, but he quickly established himself as one of the boys and was soon to be found propping up the bar and quoting Rodney Rude with the best of them. There was some concern about how much difficulty he would experience slipping back into his legal practice in Auckland, his language having deteriorated to the crew's level very quickly. We were lucky that these 'three wise men' slipped into the programme that easily, and they solved problems for the Steinlager Challenge and for the guys individually on many occasions.

By the end of the tour Big Red had gone from a strange beast that nobody knew much about, to a friendly, manageable yacht with such an exciting performance that we couldn't wait to do some serious racing in England.

Practising spinnaker peels. The new spinnaker is set before the old one is released.

CHAPTER FOUR

Show Your Cards, Gentlemen

Our base for the two months preceding the Whitbread race start was the sleepy little village of Hamble, tucked away in a corner of Southampton Water. For those of us who had sailed the previous race on *Lion New Zealand* it was a pseudo homecoming, as we all had a bit of a soft spot for the Hamble. George, the bank manager, was still sitting on the same chair in the same corner of the local pub and had a welcome cry of 'Hello boys, good to see you back', and we soon made contact with all the friends we had made four years previously.

We were uncertain as to where *Steinlager 2* was at this stage, as a shipping strike in England had meant that the ship carrying Big Red was being diverted to a port somewhere in Europe. While Blakey was on the phone locating Big Red, the rest of us settled into the crew-house, which went by the unlikely name of Sheepdip Cottage. The neighbours looked on with a certain amount of anxiety as a squad of young Kiwis moved in next door and immediately started a brisk game of cricket on the back lawn. Blakey discovered that *Steinlager 2* had arrived in Zeebrugge, Belgium, and was being off-loaded that afternoon, so it was drop the cricket bats and leap into a chartered plane for the short flight to Belgium.

Yachts are designed to stay in the water, it's their natural element, so it was pretty scary to see Big Red suspended 30 metres up in the air as they off-loaded her from the ship. Any time that the boat is not safely in the water, there is potential for damage; therefore, you hope the crane driver knows what he's doing and similarly that he hasn't got a hangover, nor that it's his first day on the job. There was a collective sigh of relief when she was floating free and we could look after her ourselves.

We spent the next two days working long hours in a large and dirty container terminal getting the rigs assembled and lifted into the boat. As there was no water available where she was moored, 15 very dirty and tired yachties finally set sail from Zeebrugge, happy to be on their way. After a slow, almost windless sail, we arrived back in the Hamble, where a hose and some scrubbing brushes cleaned off Zeebrugge's filth and there she stood at last — our big, red, mean racing machine, ready to do battle. We were very proud of her.

The attitude of the *Steinlager* crew was a marked contrast to the *Lion New Zealand* crew that had arrived in Hamble four years earlier. In the intervening years, many of us had married and through our association with the America's Cup and other international regattas were much more professional in our approach. As members of the *Lion* crew we were 22 young Kiwi boys full of bluff and bravado, more interested in chasing bad girls up the river and trying to drink the local pub dry than worrying about the computer programmes and sail shapes.

This time it was a much quieter crew, four years older and a bit smarter, not cocky, nor over-confident. We knew we had a special boat and deep down were

Deano at home on the end of the spinnaker pole preparing to change spinnakers.

quietly confident that we could win, but knew enough to realise that nothing is certain in this world and that it was up to us to make sure nothing went wrong. Many of our wives had flown in and this helped create a settled atmosphere among the crew, with most nights being spent at home in the crew-house rather than on a frantic drinkathon down at the local.

This was also our first chance to get a peek at some of our competitors, the people and yachts that we had been reading about for the last year. The more we looked, the better we felt about Big Red. *Rothmans* looked good and we had a healthy respect for the abilities of her crew, many of whom we had sailed against in previous regattas. We didn't know many of Pierre Fehlmann's crew this time, but we knew they would be good as Pierre doesn't miss much out in the preparations department, and *Merit* was the current race favourite with the press. However, some of the other yachts looked like they should have been starters in the race four years ago, and had obviously not learnt anything in the interim.

British hopes rested on the mega-budget Rothmans *campaign.*

But looks are not everything, and we needed to sail against some of these boats to get a feeling as to how competitive we would be. Our first chance came against *British Defender* and it was smiles all round after that encounter. The smiles got even bigger after a short duel with *Rothmans* and it was the talk of the town the next day that we had given *Rothmans* a real going over whilst running downwind with spinnakers on.

We tried to do most of our practice sailing out in the English Channel, rather than the Solent, to simulate ocean conditions as much as possible, and with only one watch doing the work on deck, as we would rarely have the full crew on deck during the Whitbread race. However, you can only practise so much, at some stage you have to say, 'Let's get out there and go racing'.

The first race we entered was a 180-mile sprint out into the English Channel and back, which was part of the Admiral's Cup series. No other Whitbread maxis

Defending champion Pierre Fehlmann lined up for his fourth Whitbread at the helm of Merit, *the pre-race favourite.*

were entered, but there was the good 'round-the-buoys' maxi *Congere* to line up against, as well as Dirk Nauta's smaller Whitbread entry *Equity & Law.*

Much to our delight we won the race easily on both line and handicap, and this was exactly what we needed. All systems worked well and it was a great morale booster. It was significant for us too that we beat the New Zealand Admiral's Cup yachts on handicap, a fact that we didn't forget to point out to them on numerous occasions. They took this badly, but got their revenge a few days later when they trounced us at cricket in a friendly match designed to relax everybody and give us all a day away from sailing.

The win in the Channel race didn't really mean much, but it made us a lot more confident when it came to the Fastnet Classic — a race that did mean something. Most of the Whitbread fleet had entered so this was going to be our first real test. Even though it was an important race we were determined to race in full 'Whitbread mode' and to use it as part of our training. We wanted to keep our racing sails perfect

We always felt that if we could beat F & P we would win the race.

for the Whitbread start so we used all our old training sails for the Fastnet. Similarly, we raced with only the Whitbread crew on board so we could test out the watch system we had devised. Some of the other boats took it a lot more seriously, using all new sails and importing up to ten or so extra crew to help sail the boat. This made it pretty hard at times, especially when we were alongside one of our competitors and couldn't help but compare our tired old sails to their flash new Kevlar 'fruit'. We were consoled by the thought that if we could keep up with them using our old rags then we had something up our sleeve.

We were still slightly apprehensive as to how our boatspeed would compare with the sloops, such as *Merit* and *Rothmans,* while beating into the wind, so there was no shortage of butterflies on board as we motored out for the start. The whole accent of our sail-testing programme had been reaching and running, with only a small proportion of upwind testing. All this preyed heavily on our minds before the race and we were much relieved when it immediately became obvious after the start

The first-ever Soviet entry, the radical Fazisi. *Her banana shape made for a wet ride on deck, fitting for a boat that looked like a U-boat down below.*

The start of the Fastnet was a light-airs affair and from the first minute the Kiwi ketches were locked in combat.

that we could hang in there relatively easily. We were quite happy as we left the Solent and beat along the southern English coastline. The tidal gates and local breezes were to negate any slight advantages anybody had in boatspeed and the positions in the fleet changed quite drastically as one boat got it right and leapfrogged into the lead only to lose it at the next headland if they put one foot wrong. This is one area where Kiwis struggle a bit, as we don't have a lot of experience in sailing in strong tidal conditions. The English and Europeans seemed to get it right more often than we did.

We rounded Land's End just on dark and then bashed our way upwind through the night across the Irish Sea towards the famous Fastnet Rock. To our delight the locals got this bit all wrong and it was *F & P* and Big Red first and second as dawn broke, and Fastnet Rock loomed out of the mist. Dalts and his boys had done a real job on us overnight. Obviously he had his boat smoking upwind using new sails and a big crew, and led us to the rock by five miles. Only a boatlength behind *Steinlager* came the British entry *Rothmans,* helmed by our arch-rival Lawrie 'Smoker' Smith, and she in turn had the Swiss boat *Merit* snapping at her heels.

It was pretty exciting stuff — at least Peter Montgomery thought so. Blakey had invited Peter to join the crew for the Fastnet Classic, in order to report live to radio listeners back home. Every New Zealander knows Monty's voice. It ranges from monosyllabic serious to a frenzied rush that makes yachting sound like a cross between

Rothmans skipper, Lawrie 'Smoker' Smith, with part-time crew member, Lord Lichfield. *The Kiwi boats were definitely not 'flavour of the month' with Lawrie.*

a heavyweight boxing match and the Grand National.

Approaching Fastnet Rock Monty's excitement level increased exponentially until, as we rounded with *Rothmans* right on our stern, he was really working himself into a lather. Monty was rushing around the boat seemingly unable to decide whether to take pictures of us, the yacht, the Fastnet Rock, Peter Blake, *Rothmans* or all of the above at the same time. Monty is immensely popular with all the boys and we love it when he goes into a frenzy. You've just got to sit back, relax and enjoy the show.

For some reason *F & P* made a very wide turn around the rock, so we cut it very fine and said, 'Thanks very much, we'll have half a mile back'. There followed a fast reach to Bishop Rock, the next turning mark, during which we gradually ate away at *F & P*'s lead. It was time to see if our policy of an emphasis on downwind testing was correct. Would we really 'blow them away' downwind as we had hoped? The radar was used continuously to monitor the distance between ourselves, *F & P* and the sloops. We were pleased to see the sloops, *Merit* and *Rothmans,* slipping out the back door fast, but the 'white shark' in front of us was coming back oh so slowly. Still we were gaining and it was a source of continual excitement as Brad called out the gradually reducing distance between us.

Approaching the famous Fastnet Rock off the south coast of Ireland.

Big Red approaches the finish-line off Plymouth with F & P safely tucked away.

Another sharp turn around the reefs at Bishop Rock in the middle of the night, nearly giving Mike heart failure in the process, reduced the margin by another half a mile. Suddenly *F & P* was so close we could see the instrument lights glowing in her cockpit. Baying like bloodhounds with the scent of victory in our nostrils we closed in on her for the kill. But there was no way the *F & P* boys were going to let us through. They were just as desperate and determined as we were to win this one. For the next 65 miles a hard-fought battle raged, with *Steinlager 2* attacking again and again, and *F & P* defending vigorously, each time holding us off.

After a six-hour battle Big Red finally caught one little wave, got her nose in front, cut Dalts off and slammed the door shut. We could see Grant's shoulders drop as we edged in front, but he stood up again, rallied his troops and attacked us with a gybing duel across the mouth of Plymouth Harbour, where the race was to finish. That finish-line couldn't come soon enough as far as we were concerned, and it was an anxious ten miles before we finally slipped across the line two minutes 50 seconds ahead of the 'white shark'.

The tension on both boats was released at the sound of the finishing gun, and it was two friendly Kiwi crews who came to slake their thirst in the bars of Plymouth.

We were impressed with Tracy Edwards's tenacity and determination in getting the first-ever all-woman crew to the start-line.

The Europeans seem to have different priorities to Kiwis at the end of an ocean race. The first thing they want is a shower and a good meal, whereas the average Kiwi yachtie can't seem to find enough holes in his head to pour rum and Coke down. Some of the locals looked a bit concerned as their favourite watering hole was invaded by 30 young colonials hell-bent on having a good time. They didn't seem to appreciate songs such as:

> As I was walking down the Old Kent Road into a pub I was lured,
> 'Where do you come from?' said a nosy Pom as I downed the amber fluid.
> 'I'll tell ya straight, I'm a Kiwi mate, and I feel like getting plastered,
> 'cause the beer tastes crook and the sheilas all look like you, ya Pommy bastard'.

Ross was the first one to make it back to Big Red, ostensibly on boat-security duty, but he failed to negotiate the ladder downstairs and fell about two-and-a-half metres onto the floor. Deciding that was as good a place as any to sleep, there he remained. Thereafter the rest of the crew came back in dribs and drabs, each one staggering down the ladder, standing on Ross and then flopping into the nearest bunk. Those who missed their footing at least had Ross to land on so they were saved from further injury.

The next morning we were amused to see Andrew (Raw Meat) Taylor from the *F & P* crew jump out of one of the bunks, dust himself off and with the comment, 'Nice bunks fellas', disappear up the hatch. So much for Ross's security patrol. His only comment on the matter was a confused 'I don't know what happened to me last night but I'm black and blue all over'.

The Fastnet result was one of our most satisfying wins. We were clearly very fast downwind and if any of the crews on the sloops had entertained thoughts of beating the ketches, then that race must have put the fear of God into them. At that stage the writing was on the wall in very large, very bright colours. Things had obviously changed between *Steinlager 2* and *F & P* since we had trialled in Auckland. *F & P*'s crew had apparently worked hard on her upwind speed, perceiving this as a ketch's weakness, to the detriment of her downwind performance. Not only were

All smiles after our first big win.

they disappointed at losing the race, but they were shocked at how much speed they were lacking downhill.

In retrospect, maybe we showed our hand a bit soon, as it enabled Dalts to embark immediately on a new spinnaker and mizzen staysail testing programme and over the next couple of weeks they closed the speed gap considerably. The next time they appeared on the track, they were sporting staysails that looked remarkably similar to our fastest shapes.

In the weeks after our Fastnet win there seemed to be a general animosity growing towards the ketches, not only from our sloop-rigged competitors but from the race committee also. This was typified by the problems we had with the mizzen forestays. We had made them exactly to Bruce Farr's design and hadn't for a moment thought they would be illegal. However, we heard on the grapevine that somebody was going to question them so we initiated some discussion with the race committee and the English measurers as to the forestays' legality. They seemed unable to give us an answer; therefore, we asked the head of the rules committee in America, Ken Weller, for a ruling. After a wait of some weeks we were appalled, to say the least, when Ian Bailey-Wilmot from the Whitbread race committee came down the dock waving Weller's ruling in his hand, angrily accusing us of 'trying to put one over him' and stating that 'the bloody mizzen is going to fall down anyway'. There was an offended silence on board as 14 big, bronzed Kiwis turned around to give him the evil eye. Maybe he likes hospital food, but only a restraining hand saved him from getting a bang on the nose.

Nobody seemed to be able to work out how we got such a big boat with such a large sail plan, and in spite of being measured *seven* times by New Zealand and English measurers there were still some mutterings. We just turned our back on them, confident in the knowledge that we were squeaky clean when it came to rules and that they didn't have a leg to stand on. The irony of it was that we were probably the most legal yacht there. Compared with other Whitbread entries the two Kiwi syndicates stood out like sore thumbs in terms of looks, preparation and performance, so it was natural for the others to try and take us down. Still, when somebody accuses you of cheating, it hits right to the heart.

To their credit the race committee took a very strong stance with regards to rules' compliance whilst racing, and made sure that each crew member attended a briefing, outlining his or her responsibilities with regard to shifting weight around the yacht at sea. Our friend Bailey-Wilmot was to the fore again, insisting that he was going to come out and check all the yachts while they were at sea. There were a few jokes about whales and albatrosses with Sony Handycams as we wondered how he was going to achieve this threat.

Our physical preparation for the race continued with Trae waking everyone at 6.30 each morning and guiding us on a run around the local air force base, or perhaps inviting us to partake in an aerobic circuit he had established on the back lawn of the crew-house. Thus, the neighbours woke each morning to the dulcet tones of grunting press-ups and clanking weights, combined with more than the occasional four-letter word, rugby ball or cricket ball floating over their fence. However, they didn't seem to mind and everybody was on the best of terms.

A week before the start of the Whitbread race, *Steinlager 2* was shifted to Town Quay in Southampton, and for the first time all the Whitbread entries were gathered in one place. All that was left to do was to check and double-check we had everything on board that we would need. Fifteen people had to live for the next month in a space only 25 x 5.5 metres, and had to be entirely self-sufficient for that time. There was no dropping down to the corner shop for some aspirin once we started. All the preparation had been done and the research and planning completed. It was time to get out there and give it our best shot.

Skippers assemble at pre-race briefing.
Front row, from left: *Peter Blake* (Steinlager 2), *Roger Nilson* (The Card), *Tracy Edwards* (Maiden), *Jan Santana* (Fortuna Extra Lights), *Bruno Dubois* (Rucanor Sport), *Alexei Grishenko* (Fazisi), *Andrew Coghill* (With Integrity).
Second row, from left: *Dirk Nauta* (Equity & Law II), *Lt-Col. Frank Esson* (British Defender), *Markku Wiikeri* (Martela), *Skip Novak* (Fazisi), *Alain Gabbay* (Charles Jourdan), *Dr Jochen Orgelmann* (Schlussel Von Bremen).
Back row, from left: *Grant Dalton* (Fisher & Paykel), *Harry Harkimo* (Belmont Finland), *Joe English* (NCB Ireland), *Daniel Malle* (La Poste), *John Chittenden* (Creightons Naturally), *Ludde Ingvall* (Union Bank of Finland), *Bob Salmon* (Liverpool Enterprise), *Pierre Fehlmann* (Merit), *Georgio Falck* (Gatorade).

CHAPTER FIVE

Easy Street

Arriving at Town Quay on the morning of the start was something of a shock for us after leaving the tranquillity of our crew-house half an hour earlier. Hustling our way through thousands of spectators and dozens of TV crews down to the boat was more traumatic than any of our training so far. Security guards patrolling the docks were coming in for all sorts of abuse as they attempted to keep unauthorised people away from the boats. A minor panic ensued as the docks began to sink under the weight of the media and supporters. After an hour of mayhem at the marina we were all more than happy to slip our mooring lines and motor out into the Solent to ready ourselves for the start.

After the crowds at Town Quay it was a relief to have an hour to collect our thoughts and prepare the boat for sailing. Blakey gave us our final crew briefing as we waited to hoist the sails — the message was clear, we had a fast boat with nine months' solid preparation behind us and now it was up to us, the crew, to make sure we got the result the boat was worthy of.

This leg of the race was always going to be the most important. A good result to Punta would set us up for the whole race and, conversely, a bad result would have us on our back foot for the remainder of the race, forever trying to make up that time. Therefore, 75 per cent of Mike's pre-race research applied to the first leg.

This leg was going to be difficult because the course would take us straight south through several major weather systems, from tradewinds to the notorious doldrums, more tradewinds and then an area of variables before reaching Uruguay.

The time of reckoning finally arrived and as the Duke of York fired the cannon to signal the start of this marathon we spat out of the bunch like an orange pip, with five sails set. In a 15-knot northerly breeze it wasn't long before we asserted our dominance over the 23-boat fleet to lead by a couple of minutes from F & P. The Solent was more akin to the Tongariro River in flood than its usual more placid self as hundreds of spectator boats churned up the water in an attempt to keep up with the leaders effortlessly sailing down towards the Needles at 13 knots.

Shortly before leaving the Solent we set our flat Mylar reaching spinnaker in response to F & P setting theirs astern of us. No sooner had we set our spinnaker than we were headed by the wind and had to hurriedly rehoist our jib top and drop the spinnaker as we careered towards the shore. F & P's brace came unclipped off the spinnaker at the same time, so our lead was preserved.

As the spectator fleet turned around one by one and returned to Southampton we settled into the business of yacht racing. The last spectator boat to leave us out in the English Channel had a large group of Kiwis on board obviously enjoying more than a few Steinlagers. They performed a haka which reminded us that we weren't just in this for ourselves — we had a whole country behind us back home. By dusk

Home away from home for a bowman 30 metres up the rig.

we still held the lead with *F & P* one mile dead astern and the sloops even further behind. Little did we know the pecking order for the next nine months had already been established.

The next morning we were off Ushant on the north-west corner of France. This landmark is a notorious tidal gate separating the Bay of Biscay from the English Channel. We were a little wary of sailing through this tidal gate as at this stage on the 1985/86 Whitbread *Cote d'Or*, skippered by the legendary Frenchman Eric Tabarly, had been caught by a foul tide there and had lost ten hours on the fleet. However, this time we had six knots of favourable current with us and as we sailed through with a spinnaker set in light airs the water was boiling as it forced its way through the narrow channel.

Daylight revealed that *Rothmans, Merit* and *Union Bank of Finland (UBF)* had done a number on us by sailing closer to the French coast and led us through the channel by five miles. Once clear of the coast and sailing south across the Bay of Biscay with a light spinnaker and our big white staysail set, we slowly but surely reeled the sloops in. We sailed through the lee of *UBF* going 0.75 of a knot faster, which in ocean racing is comparable to a Ferrari going past a Mini. *UBF*'s skipper, Ludde

'Get rid of it!' Goddy prepares to trip the spinnaker away.

Ingvall, unable to watch us sailing by, went down below and got into his bunk, pulling his blanket over his head in the hope that it was all a bad dream. It wasn't only Ludde who had to live the nightmare as we did exactly the same to 'Marty' Fehlmann's Swiss crew aboard *Merit*. It was at this stage that Brad was interviewed on the helm, telling the video camera, 'Marty's got a dog — we're fast!' Unbeknown to Brad that particular piece of footage was to be shown worldwide on the television networks.

For a few hours that afternoon we had an unusual visitor on board in the form of a bat. It made itself at home hanging around in the rig for a few hours. After much conjecture we decided it was probably on a spy mission for Bailey-Wilmot with a microfilm camera attached to it checking up that we weren't cheating.

With the sloops now astern and 'Fishpie', as we called *F & P*, a comfortable 16 miles behind, we enjoyed perfect conditions all the way across the Bay of Biscay with all our heavy artillery on display — spinnaker and big red mizzen staysail. The only drama occurred when a large whale surfaced off our starboard bow, forcing us to luff up sharply to avoid the leviathan as it disappeared beneath us. Scary memories of whale bashing and a broken rudder on *Lion New Zealand* die hard.

About this time, the log records that 'Brad is having problems with the consistency of his daily runs'. Dr Mungbean was called upon to issue some pills to rectify the problem and showed very little sympathy; his bedside manner was becoming more like that of a real doctor by the day.

As we approached Cape Finisterre off the northwest corner of Spain during our third night at sea, we were soon shaken out of our dream-ride when we were confronted with 40-knot tailwinds which, combined with big seas, heavy shipping and a moonless night had us all pumped up on adrenalin. With the wind increasing in strength very quickly, we had been caught out with a full-size spinnaker and a small, red, heavy-duty mizzen spinnaker set. Ross was on the helm at the time and as the boat teetered on the edge of control, blasting along at a solid 19 knots, his voice raised a few octaves as he yelled *'GET IT OOOFFF!!!'*. With a smaller, more manageable spinnaker set and a reefed mainsail we surfed through the darkness constantly monitoring the radar for shipping. At one stage a large tanker, having observed us with spotlights illuminating our sails, did a 360° turn to avoid us.

At daybreak we spotted a sail on the western horizon which, sailing on a converging course, turned out to be *Rothmans*. While we continued heading out to sea on starboard gybe under an 85 per cent spinnaker and reefed mainsail, *Rothmans* crossed our stern on port gybe only two boatlengths behind with a poled-out headsail set. With both boats surfing in excess of 20 knots and spray flying everywhere, it was a spectacular sight. In contrast to previous Whitbreads, close encounters between boats at sea such as this were to become a feature of this race. Unbeknown to us at the time, this splitting of direction was to prove to be our big break on the rest of the fleet in this leg and ultimately the race.

While the on-watch crew were 'white-knuckling' the boat with as much sail set as possible, Blakey and Mike were equally tense in the nav station poring over the maps which were constantly feeding out of the weather fax. Mike was running the weather maps through the Apple Macwinds routing programme, which was agreeing with their gut feeling that a westerly course was the way to go. *Merit* was following suit while the rest of the maxis had opted to stay close to the Portuguese coast. We weren't unhappy heading west as that was according to our pre-race game plan; also the computer, weather maps and our own logic said that was the correct decision as we were sailing down a 'river' of wind which was the only breeze in town. We were a little nervous as this put us out on a bit of a limb being the most westerly boat, but we couldn't understand why more of our opposition weren't doing the same. At one stage a worried Mike wanted to gybe back in and re-establish contact with the rest of the fleet, but Blakey said, 'No, it's logical. What we are doing is right, let's stick to our guns'. Much to our excitement it wasn't long before our decision began to pay dividends as we managed to hold on to a stronger breeze out to the west while the boats to the east were stuck in a lightening breeze.

By day six the gale had abated completely and we were once more sailing

'Go west young man.' Fast sailing off Cape Finisterre — Shoebie steers while Jaws trims the spinnaker. The mizzen was lowered when the wind got over 40 knots.

downwind in light-to-moderate airs. With *Merit* 30 miles astern and a huge gap back to *Rothmans* and Fishpie, we were in good shape. We were quietly confident that if the moderate running continued we'd ease away from *Merit*. Being out to the west we had a better angle of attack as we sailed south and over the next week built up a huge lead over the boats languishing in lighter airs inshore.

With the equator still ten days away a campaign of intimidation, for those on board who hadn't sailed across before and entered King Neptune's realm, began in earnest. These mind games of constantly psyching the rookies up for the impending line-crossing ceremony were to become a constant source of humour.

The next few days saw very consistent weather. As expected we slowly but surely stretched our legs on *Merit* and the boats further to the northeast. By now the sea and air temperature had warmed up dramatically as we neared the tropics and bucket baths on the aft deck became very popular. It wasn't long before Big Red's aft deck

The Dukes enjoy a perfect afternoon's sail through the trades.

was christened Copacabana Beach as the standby crew washed and relaxed on it. With little excitement on board, Trae came up on deck and told us that he had just had a vivid dream that he was Superman flying around the Auckland suburb of Newmarket rescuing people. However, we weren't able to find Clark Kent's phone-box on board. The general consensus was that either the freeze-dried food was starting to affect Trae's mind or that he had been delving into his medical supplies and taking something mildly hallucinogenic.

By the end of our first week at sea we had sailed 1900 miles and were well to the southwest of the Canary Islands, which on the old course to Cape Town we would have sailed through. It was most unusual that apart from the reach down the Solent at the start we had been flying a spinnaker for 1900 miles — we certainly were not complaining. At 26° North the breeze began to increase slowly again to 20 knots, which was diagnosed as the tradewinds developing.

Once into the steady tradewind conditions the standby watch were rarely called on deck and spent most of their time sleeping on the sails in the companionway down below, charging their batteries for the inevitable sail-changing frenzy the doldrums would provide us. Obviously we were still getting the better of the conditions as our lead continued to build. By day nine we had a comfortable 80-mile lead over *Merit* while Dalts and his boys were having a tough time, now 205 miles astern. On the inter-yacht sched Dalts asked Blakey what the weather was like in the tropics, claiming they still had their snowsuits on up north.

In these balmy conditions by far the greatest hazard to the crew were the flying fish which were indiscriminately bombarding the guys on deck. Their tactics were most effective at night when a cry of horror could be heard as someone got 'slimed' by a kamikaze flying fish. It was most disconcerting when on the helm to observe a squadron of flying fish soaring across the deck illuminated by our navigation lights. You knew it wasn't going to be long before your number was up. Even so, the sensation of a flying fish slamming into the side of your face was not a pleasant one. Even worse was when Grim got hit in the family jewels by a large flying fish travelling at an estimated 400 miles per hour — 'Ouch!'. The smell left behind by these projectiles was terrible and was very difficult to get out of your hair and clothing, suddenly making you unpopular with the rest of the crew.

On day ten the breeze finally headed us, and our cake ride under spinnaker came to an end as we hoisted our reaching headsails. By this stage we had extended our lead over Fishpie to a whopping 270 miles. They must have been hating life as we surely would have, had the roles been reversed. Our confidence was soon eroded as the next day the breeze swung through to the south and crumped right away, leaving us totally becalmed. Our position was 11° 30' North, so we assumed we had encountered the doldrums and knew that the other boats would soon approach the same conditions. Not so — it proved to be our very own calm patch, the result of Hurricane Hugo in its infancy to the west of us. While we had been sitting becalmed, our opposition, including *Merit,* had continued on down-track unabated at 10 knots. The midday sched was 'scary movies' for us as *Merit* pulled up to within

40 miles after our incredibly frustrating 12-hour run of only 28 miles. It's on days like these the crew's mettle is really tested. After getting over the initial frustration and muttering a few obscenities about 'Huey', the Kiwi yachtman's Wind God, you soon put it behind and adopt an attitude of 'Well that was a bummer, but let's pull finger and go get our lead back again'.

The extreme heat was starting to make life down below pretty uncomfortable. With a sadistic touch BC even served us chilli con carne for lunch one day which resulted in the guys all breaking out into bouts of perspiration. Big Red's ventilation down below was not great. In the continuing attempts to save weight, we had decided against bunk fans, the wisdom of which we began to question as we lay sweating bucket-loads on our bunks and attempting to sleep. To combat the problem of fluid loss, Trae had brought along a limited supply of salt tablets. These disappeared very quickly, resulting in fingers being pointed in all directions in an attempt to find the culprit.

Having been stung a couple of days earlier, there was a lot of tension and nervousness in the air when we finally did encounter the doldrums. Had we bought tickets to our own private parking lot again? Or had the opposition run into calms

A flying fish's view of Steinlager 2.

also? The doldrums, technically referred to as the Inter Tropical Convergence Zone (ITCZ), are an area where the northeast tradewinds of the northern hemisphere clash with the southeasterly trades of the southern hemisphere. It is a very volatile area of quickly changing conditions, characterised by towering cumulonimbus thunderheads complete with violent thunderstorms. It is always a bit of a gamble as to which point you choose to enter the doldrums, but fortunately the next sched revealed that although *Merit* had nearly caught up to us again, they were also into the doldrums. The only positive aspect of the doldrums are the frequent rain showers which provide a welcome opportunity for a luxurious freshwater wash and hair shampoo which leaves you feeling great for half an hour until the benefits are ruined by another dose of heavy perspiration.

Little did we know at the time that we actually managed to escape from the doldrums in good shape, whereas the boats a day astern of us didn't have things

King Neptune, alias BC, arrives on board to preside over his court.

quite so easy. With the biggest obstacle of the leg behind us, attention was turned to the imminent equator crossing and the rookies were becoming justifiably apprehensive. In preparation for the line-crossing ceremonies BC had been nurturing a bucket of swill consisting of leftover food scraps with a little yeast to help it along.

Brad, sensing that perhaps he was in for the hardest time, wrote in the log, 'I feel danger lurks in every corner, what will tomorrow bring?'. He didn't have to wait long as the next morning shortly after crossing the equator the mood was set as 'Phantom of the Opera' boomed over the stereo, signalling the beginning of proceedings. Ross's experience as a cop was called upon to prepare the charge sheet, listing the 'crimes' committed. Overseeing the ceremony was King Neptune (BC) and Grim as an unlikely Queen Codfish, resplendent with the necessary accessories, but looking more like a bear in drag. The crimes were read out by the prosecutor and no matter what they said, the rookies were found guilty of such inane crimes as wasting

Billy's fears of the equator crossing ceremony were well founded. King Neptune, Queen Codfish and Goddy the prosecutor appear content as justice has been done.

oxygen or others their mothers wouldn't want to know about. King Neptune decided the punishment and the executioner carried out his orders. Usually this involved a liberal dousing of swill and an alteration to their hairstyle. Once the punishments had been administered the new subjects of Neptune's realm were untied and we resumed the business of yacht racing.

Back into the tradewinds south of the equator life was very pleasant once more. There's something appealing about coming on watch in the middle of the night dressed only in a pair of shorts. During these periods when there are few wind changes and, therefore, few sail changes there is plenty of time to 'chill out' on the deck and tell each other stories. These tend to be about past races that we've won and lost and the antics we've got up to in various parts of the world. After the supply of stories begins to dissipate, you start to hear the same old tales over again. Barry was definitely one of the more lateral thinkers amongst the crew and on one occasion, after seeing a spectacular shooting star, he tried to engage some of his watch in a discussion on astronomy. Unfortunately, Barry's enthusiasm towards the night sky was not shared by his watch mates and it wasn't long before he was known as 'Moon the Loon'. Sometimes it didn't pay to be different.

Reaching south through the trades with our five-sail 'venetian blind' arrangement set, the Dukes came up on watch after another one of BC's culinary delights. They had only been on watch a couple of minutes when Ross, on the helm, tells Foxy, 'Retrim all the sails Glen, it's all out of whack!' This was taken as something of an insult by Shoebie's watch, who had just been relieved, and from that day on whenever anyone had the audacity to ask how the trim was, they would be greeted with a chorus of 'Perfect!'

As Big Red continued southwards making good progress through the tradewinds we felt for the crews on the maxis at the back of the fleet. Whilst the leading four boats had managed a quick escape from the doldrums, those further back were well and truly trapped as the transient doldrums moved south at the same speed as the boats. Their progress was painfully slow. The guys on NCB Ireland must have been hurting as we stretched out to a 900-mile lead on them.

By day 18, we were 7° South with Merit tucked away about 100 miles astern once more and the boys on Fishpie almost 200 miles in arrears. With today's navigation technology it is very rare to see the navigator with a sextant in his hand. However, that was soon necessary as our Satnav inconveniently broke down. Immediately, Mike broke into a cold sweat at the prospect of having to navigate by sextant. He had enough trouble just trying to figure out how to open the case. Blakey was delighted to have a real reason to have a play with his beloved sextant and spent the next two days taking sun and star shots. The problem with the Satnav was diagnosed as a burst of RF (Radio Frequency) through it, much to the navigator's relief, and it was soon reprogrammed and up and running once more.

Now that we had built up our lead over the opposition to what it was before the doldrums someone wrote in the logbook, 'Payback time — John Justice strikes back!' Throughout the race the mythical John Justice was to become our minder. Some of the F & P boys took it all to heart when Glen wrote about John Justice in

35 knots we were reeling off the miles. Sailing through the pitch black of a moonless night surfing down waves at 22 knots, the sensation is not a lot different to the Space Mountain rollercoaster ride at Disneyland.

Off Cape Finisterre earlier in the leg while blasting in similar conditions one of the guys likened the high-speed surfing to being in the 'green room', surfies' parlance for riding a tube. As huge bow waves rushed back either side of the boat high above the deck the helmsman's peripheral vision was reduced to nil. Walking around down below in these conditions as the boat rolls and surges down the seas is a little like taking a casual stroll down the aisle of a runaway San Francisco tram car. Just as we were starting to count down the days for an ETA at Punta del Este, 'Huey' turned the wind machine off, leaving us flopping around in a huge leftover seaway and no wind, making life on board very unpleasant as the booms went crashing from side to side. Ironically it's in these conditions that the potential for breakages is greatest.

However, we were not becalmed for long as a depression forming off the coast of Uruguay produced a cold front, followed by freshening southerlies, which was to give us a 600-mile 'dead maggot', the term yachties use to describe the situation where the finish-line is directly to windward. Within two hours the wind was up to 35 knots leaving us with only a triple-reefed mainsail and No. 5 genoa set, with the mizzen down completely. After the heat of the tropics the sudden cold change was

Beating into the dawn. 'Huey' wasn't going to let us win easily.

a shock to the system and as few of us had brought gloves on this leg we were forced to pull woollen socks over our hands in an attempt to keep them warm as the temperature continued to plummet.

As the seas built, *Steinlager 2* was making some horrific noises as she crashed off the back of the waves into big 'holes' in the ocean. With *Merit, Rothmans* and Dalton's crowd safely tucked away, Peter wisely decided to drop the headsail and nurse the boat along at slower speeds to ensure we finished intact. Lawrie Smith on *Rothmans,* desperate to try and close the gap on us, was pushing hard into the gale. Too hard, he was soon to find out as they crashed particularly hard off one wave, cracking the deck beside the running backstay winch and forcing them to back off also. We'd had such a fantastic ride so far through the leg that 'Huey' decided to make us work hard for each of the remaining 500 miles to the finish.

Progress was painfully slow in these conditions. Sleeping was almost impossible with the banging and crashing, and on deck it was wet and cold. Roll on Punta! With less than 200 miles to go 'Huey' set us one more test when the mainsail fell away from the headboard car, which pulls the sail up and down the mast. In near-impossible conditions Goddy and Shoebie went aloft with the boat-hook taped to a length of sail batten to try to retrieve the headboard car and reconnect it to the mainsail. Luckily they were successful on their first attempt and we were able to rehoist the mainsail and wind Big Red back up to full speed again.

Because we encountered the southerly gale first we lost time to *Merit*, who had closed back to within 80 miles of us as we sailed along the featureless Uruguayan coast and into Punta del Este. We finally crossed the finish-line off the small harbour in Punta at 0500 hours local time on a cold, blustery morning. We were ecstatic; after 6281 miles we had come through with the first-ever Kiwi win on a Whitbread leg and, although we did not fully appreciate it at the time, we had established a comfortable buffer zone which was to set us up for the remainder of the race. After ingesting vast quantities of Steinlager and premixed gin and tonics we had some trouble finding our way home. In fact, some didn't even make it. Peter Montgomery left it too late to interview Mike, who was already having trouble getting his sentences out. After removing all of the slurred four-letter words Peter found himself left with a lot of um's and aahh's.

It was not until later that day that we discovered that Fishpie had lost her mizzen rig in the strong tailwinds off Rio. We felt for Dalts's boys, but after all the close racing we'd had in England, it was beyond our wildest dreams to have an advantage of this magnitude so early in the race. We reflected on a successful leg where we had not only beaten *Merit* by 11½ hours but had accumulated almost 32 hours on F & P, which we always considered to be our most dangerous rival.

Pierre Fehlmann and his Merit *crew can still manage a smile, having come in 11½ hours behind us.*

Leg One: Southampton — Punta del Este (6281 miles)

Class	Boat Name	Days	Elapsed Time Hours	Mins	Secs	Finishing Position	Handicap Position
A	*Steinlager 2*	25	20	46	27	1	1
A	*Merit*	26	8	11	20	2	2
A	*Fisher & Paykel NZ*	27	3	50	26	3	3
A	*Rothmans*	27	7	20	0	4	4
A	*The Card*	28	6	43	25	5	5
A	*Fazisi*	28	13	20	18	6	7
A	*Gatorade*	28	13	22	58	7	6
A	*Martela O.F.*	28	13	54	58	8	8
A	*British Defender*	28	14	23	52	9	10
A	*Fortuna Extra Lights*	28	19	49	45	10	9
A	*Charles Jourdan*	28	20	10	18	11	11
A	*Belmont Finland II*	28	20	21	15	12	12
A	*NCB Ireland*	29	5	27	46	13	13
A	*Union Bank of Finland*	29	13	49	5	14	15
C	*Equity & Law II*	31	22	28	36	15	14
A	*Liverpool Enterprise*	32	3	15	55	16	19
CRUISE	*Creightons Naturally*	34	7	59	15	17	22
D	*L'Esprit de Liberte*	34	9	2	59	18	17
D	*Rucanor Sport*	34	10	20	3	19	16
D	*Maiden*	35	0	46	44	20	18
D	*Schlussel Von Bremen*	35	5	46	37	21	20
CRUISE	*With Integrity*	35	7	11	47	22	23
D	*La Poste*	37	20	4	18	23	21

Changes In Latitudes, Changes In Attitudes

Punta del Este is the seasonal Riviera of South America. It was a very different resort town that we arrived at than the Punta we remembered from our stop on *Lion New Zealand* in the 1985/86 Whitbread race. Throughout the summer it becomes the playground of wealthy Argentinians, many of whom commute by aircraft from Buenos Aires to spend the weekend.

However, when we arrived it was still early spring and Punta took on the appearance of a ghost town, with only a few of the abundant restaurants and shops open. Our accommodation was in a high-rise apartment block called the Lafayette. It was no time at all before it was nicknamed 'the Laugh-at-it'. Because of the close proximity of the apartments to the boat and nearby restaurants, we commuted everywhere by foot. This was considerably safer than driving with the excitable Latin Americans who tend to make up the road rules as they go along.

Throughout our stay in Punta the crews were prohibited from using the exclusive yacht club. This we could live with, but when local officials even barred us from using the nearby yacht club annex, restricting it to the media, there was a lot of ill-feeling amongst the crews. We were beginning to feel like second-class citizens and wondered for whom exactly the Uruguayans were hosting the stopover. It wasn't long before we all ignored the signs and began patronising the annex bar and restaurant anyway.

As the weather was not too conducive to swimming at any of Punta's magnificent beaches we turned our attention to the Cantegril Country Club. During our stay in Punta four years earlier, the country club had invited us to use their facilities and the same privileges were to apply this time. As well as the gym, the club's facilities included ten clay tennis courts, a large swimming pool and a nearby golf course.

It was the golf course that was to attract much of the crew's enthusiasm. After finishing work on the boat for the day, there would be a dash out to the golf course to play a few holes. As with any competitive sportsmen, we couldn't just play for fun and before long a golf tournament was organised amongst the *Steinlager* crew. As the designated day arrived, we all drew lots for partners and competed for overall honours around the superb 18-hole course. Quickly it became evident who the hot-shots amongst the crew were and with total disregard to golfing etiquette it was compulsory to drink a Steinie periodically throughout the tournament.

At the end of the day Shoebie and Mike won amidst a fury of cheating accusations over their arithmetic. Undoubtedly, the most entertaining pair were Blakey and Baz. At the first tee, Blakey confidently addressed the ball and promptly sliced

Fog and mist were our constant companions.

it into a nearby backyard patrolled by a large, ferocious Doberman. From that point on mutterings could be heard, such as 'mumble, mumble, stupid bloody game'. Meanwhile Baz would line up 15 perfect practice swings, step up to the ball and instantly seize into a Rambo pose, determined to try and launch the ball into the ionosphere. Unfortunately Baz's club, travelling at close to the speed of light, usually connected with the turf 15 centimetres behind the ball. He worked his way around the beautiful golf course with all the grace of a Caterpillar bulldozer, excavating a few new bunkers along the fairways.

Between our hectic golf and tennis schedule we worked on the boat, replacing all of the running rigging and many of the sails. The riggers gave both the mizzen and main mast thorough checks for any possible cracks or fatigue in the fittings. With what was undoubtedly the longest and hardest leg across the desolate waters of the Southern Ocean ahead of us, we had to make absolutely sure that Big Red was in a 100 per cent state of readiness.

Rothmans skipper, Lawrie Smith, flew back to England during the stopover and was quoted in the British press calling us cheats on the basis that 'no-one has ever seen Blake's boat out of the water'. We were not sure quite what he expected to

The ever-present Uruguayan crowd watches the sloop-rigged F & P *arrive third into Punta.*

find on our keel. In retrospect, Smith was probably just trying to unsettle us, but in reality, all he achieved by this accusation was to make us even more determined to beat him. All the same, we were not enjoying Smith's broadsides, and on a few occasions embarrassed *Rothmans* crew members came up to us in Punta and apologised for their skipper's comments.

We soon learnt that when you win by a margin as big as ours on the first leg, it is hard to be popular with everyone. One foreign journalist even commented in Punta that the *Steinlager* crew were so well behaved that they were 'bordering on being boring'. This was just an indication that we all enjoyed each other's company, as a close-knit team does, and did not have to tear around town for entertainment.

During our stay in Punta we got to know two of the Soviet *Fazisi* crew quite well. Crocodile and Serge spoke limited English and with a stopover in Auckland to come, they were keen to learn some typical Kiwi expressions. After a couple of lessons, they were soon slotting phrases such as 'No worries mate', 'You beauty!' and 'Shit yeah' into their vocabularies, more often than not completely out of context.

With the Southern Ocean ahead of us everything on the boat was checked and double-checked. Clutch was in charge of servicing the deck gear.

The *Fazisi* crew were to suffer a tragic shock when their skipper Alexei Grishenko committed suicide, hanging himself in the woods just out of town. Initially there was speculation that *Fazisi* would pull out of the race, but fortunately they were to continue. Without a doubt, the worst tragedy occurred when Janne Gustafsson, a very popular Swedish crewman on *The Card,* was killed in a motorcycle accident a week before we were due to leave Punta.

On the morning of the re-start we cast our mooring lines ashore to Jaapi, our shore manager, and said 'adios' to the land of giant steaks and 'cafe con leche' and started to focus our thoughts on the leg to Fremantle. An hour before the start, every boat tossed a simple wreath into the sea in memory of Janne. For those of us who had known Janne when he had crewed aboard *Drum* in the previous Whitbread it was especially sad to see his life drift away with that wreath.

However, we did not have long to mull on that thought as we hoisted our new sails in preparation for the start. Vivid memories of apprehensive anticipation, as we left Cape Town four years ago on *Lion New Zealand* to head into the unknown Southern Ocean, came flooding back as we circled our opposition, waiting for the start gun to fire. The Duchess of York was to fire the cannon and the *Steinlager* crew had all felt privileged to have met her a couple of days earlier when she visited our boat.

Blakey and Brad managed to get us another good start as Fergie sent us on our way and we were not surprised when we heard over the VHF radio that F & P had started prematurely and had to return and restart again, losing 15 valuable minutes for their troubles. As we reached along to the first turning mark three miles up the coast we were accompanied by a sizable spectator fleet, all intent on getting in for the closest look and displaying characteristic Latin American enthusiasm.

Leading the fleet away from Punta out into the South Atlantic we found ourselves in a rapidly freshening breeze. By nightfall on the first day the wind had swung aft to give us a nerve-racking night blasting downwind under spinnaker at speeds in excess of 20 knots. Any thoughts of a gentle start to the leg were soon abandoned. Many of the crew had caught a virus during the stopover, which was slowing everyone down a bit and did nothing for our performance or morale.

It soon became apparent that this leg was going to be much closer racing than the first, when we had enjoyed a comfortable lead. The ketches held an advantage over the sloops in moderate conditions when we could set our extra sail area on the mizzen. Obviously the considerably lighter sloops were going to be an altogether tougher proposition in the heavy-air, down-wind sailing that is the trademark of the Southern Ocean.

Before leaving the relative warmth of Punta, Mike had set out our strategy for this leg. The great circle course which would take us on the shortest route to Fremantle would see us heading southeast from Punta for about a week until we were into the depths of the Southern Ocean and had reached the latitude at which we intended to sail across the bottom of the world. The limiting factor for the distance we would travel south was the Antarctic pack ice, which, at this time of the year, was as far

north as it ever comes. After spending two weeks sailing eastwards through the Southern Ocean, the game plan was to gradually start our ascent to Fremantle, once clear of the Kerguelen Islands. The final hurdle would be to negotiate the large area of high pressure which is usually found off the southwest coast of Australia.

A Whitbread crewman's worst nightmare is to be caught on the wind in the Southern Ocean. And on day three, this was exactly what happened. As we bashed to weather in the teeth-chattering conditions a few of us decided that perhaps golf is a more sensible sport after all. Our misery was compounded as Fishpie and the two 'cigarette boats', *Rothmans* and *Merit,* had made a sizable jump on us by sailing a more southerly course which was giving them a freer breeze as a result of a low-pressure system.

These low-pressure systems were relatively small and if you were in the wrong place, boats 20 miles on either side could encounter vastly differing conditions and march ahead. Tacticians often talk of being 'in phase' with the wind shifts and for the first week of this leg, as we headed southwards, that is something we were definitely not, as we seemed to be forever behind the eight ball, losing valuable ground to the leading three boats. Our biggest mistake had been that we hadn't headed south as aggressively as *F & P.*

Fergie was a big hit with the boys during our stopover in Punta del Este.

By the end of our first week at sea, the weather had cooled dramatically with the water temperature down to a bracing 3°C and the air temperature no warmer. Two days earlier an RAF Hercules had flown overhead. It was frustrating to think that its crew were warm and dry and would soon be back at their Falkland Islands base having a beer while we slogged it out in conditions that our log described simply as 'Yuk!'

In addition to not fitting any fans for the tropical legs, it had been decided during the planning of the boat not to fit a diesel heater. This was in order to save not only the weight of the heater but also the fuel that would be required to run it. As the interior temperature of the boat dropped to around freezing and the stark white bulkheads and deckheads gave the interior the ambience of a refrigerator, we were beginning to question our judgement. It was ironic that Fishpie was sponsored by a refrigerator manufacturer, yet they had a heating system on board. If the hatches were left open it was easy to believe you would end up as freeze-dried as our meals.

Getting dressed to go on watch in these conditions was a major ordeal. Having been woken by one of the on-watch crew dripping freezing water over your face off his wet-weather jacket with an encouraging 'It's bloody wet and cold up there

We held grave fears for Goddy's sanity sailing in his third Whitbread as a bowman.

and you're the next lucky contestant', it's time to extract yourself from your lovely warm Vitality sleeping-bag and begin to get dressed. Having slept in your polypropylene long johns, which tend to become a little uncomfortable and smelly after ten days, you pull on a woollen sweater, a fleecy-lined bodysuit and a couple of pairs of socks. Slowly you begin to warm up again with the exertion of pulling on even more layers. Next comes the waterproof, fleecy-lined jacket and leather-lined rubber sea-boots. Then you clamber into your triple-lined, wet-weather trousers and jacket with a built-in life-harness. All that remains is to pull on your balaclava and two pairs of gloves. Normally it is at about this stage of proceedings that, bearing a striking resemblance to the Michelin Man, you experience an urgent desire to go to the toilet.

The virus that we had caught in port was lingering, a symptom of which was a sore throat. Dr Mungbean's remedy for this ailment was simple — 'Have a cup of tea and a Strepsil.' With advice like this, there was little fear of anyone turning into a hypochondriac. However, Dr Mungbean did display alarm at the vast quantities of Strepsils being consumed and wrote in the log, 'I hope Strepsils are not addictive as we've just knocked off 420 and have only 24 left, so your throats had better come

With lifelines hooked on, there were no risks taken sailing down in the big chilli bin.

right quick'. He then concluded with the sort of prescription we had come to expect from him — 'Try Weet-Bix'.

Having sailed 1700 miles since leaving Punta, Big Red was still behind the leading three boats, who were enjoying more wind to the south of us. Having lost 30 miles to Dalts in a 12-hour period, there was an air of anxiety on board as Blakey, Mike and the three watch captains met around the nav station to pore over the charts and make a decision as to whether we continued on our present course in light airs and face the risk of losing more miles, or bite the bullet and gybe across onto starboard and head south in search of the fresher winds F & P was enjoying. After a short discussion it was unanimously agreed that we should gybe over to the unfavoured gybe in the hope that we could stop the rot. The hardest aspect of this decision was that it meant we would be handing F & P 20 miles on a plate. It was a case of trying to decide which was the lesser of the two evils.

Our question was answered the next day, as our game of Russian roulette had appeared to pay off, when we spotted Rothmans through the fog three miles astern of us. The next sched showed Merit and UBF off on our port beam, so we were back in the race even if we had lost time to our arch-rivals on F & P.

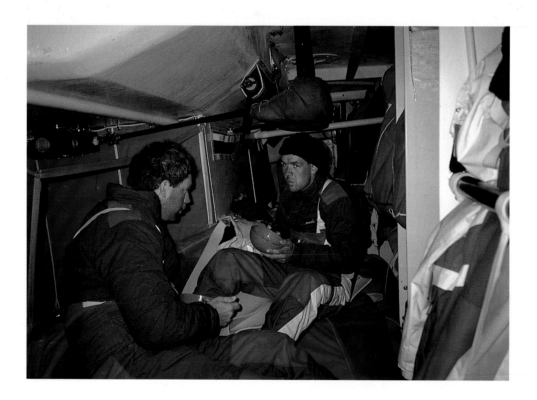

Grim and Spike share a corner table in the palatial interior of Big Red.

The Southern Ocean appears to have an abundance of whales and the whaling ban in that part of the world seems to be working. One sunny afternoon at the end of our first week at sea, a 15-metre fin whale decided to keep us company for a while. As it swam alongside us it surfaced periodically, at which times we could see its huge eyes looking at us. We were so close that as it surfaced and spouted, the spume sprayed all over the guys on deck on many occasions. An anxious hour followed as obviously the whale took perverse pleasure in making us very nervous swimming beneath the boat, rolling onto its back displaying its vast white belly. The general consensus was that the whale had a crush on Big Red and we just hoped that it did not try to consummate the relationship.

By day ten with *F & P* 55 miles ahead of us we spotted our first iceberg. Throughout the day we monitored three 'bergs on our on-deck radar screen, one of which we passed within half-a-mile in thick fog without even seeing it — not an altogether comforting sensation.

The log book was being peppered with literary gems as it gave an on-watch crew member an excuse to go down below for a few minutes every hour to record progress. Brad was the leading exponent of weird log-book entries and after passing

Freo — here we come!

one particularly large iceberg he wrote, 'Saw the All Blacks last night waving to us from the top of an iceberg, must have cost Steinlager heaps'. Another pastime that was becoming increasingly popular as the temperature became correspondingly colder was making the hot drinks in the galley during the watch. This gave the opportunity to warm frozen hands on the boiling kettle and stay down below for a few minutes.

After a few days of variables, the wind began to strengthen from the west as a result of a large low-pressure system building to the south of us. The wind built to gale-force, where it was to stay for the best part of a week. The seas continued to build in size and the ride became faster and faster. During this gale we were to discover that one of *Steinlager 2*'s Achilles heels was hard-running. There were no such concerns for the sloops, however, which being considerably lighter soon overhauled us and opened up a lead of over 50 miles. Obviously Dalts and his boys were also finding the conditions to their liking as they blasted away to a lead of over 100 miles.

A Whitbread yachtsman's biggest enemy at sea is 'downtime'. This is the time spent repairing damage to the boat; therefore, the boat is not being sailed at maximum efficiency and is consequently losing miles. With the gale unrelenting, we were breaking our fair share of gear. It was very frustrating, considering the amount of work and preparation that had gone into the boat during our stay in Punta, which by now seemed a distant memory.

Our problems began when the spinnaker halyard blocks failed, with the result that the wire spinnaker halyards were badly damaged, and while one of the blocks was thrashing around it tore a hole in the mainsail. This had to be lowered to the deck for two hours so the sailmakers could repair it. By the end of this expensive episode there were a few blue words being muttered about the manufacturer of these blocks. To add insult to injury, the track, to which the inboard end of the spinnaker pole is fastened, shattered, calling for a few rugby skills to try and tackle the thrashing spinnaker pole and bring it under control.

Our demolition derby was rounded off when our hydraulic main boom vang broke as the boom was dragged through the freezing seas. Peter and Baz had a go at repairing it and Blakey was so confident of the integrity of the repair that he boldly stated that he would 'walk home naked if it breaks again'. The next day the vang *did* break again, leading to much excitement amongst the crew, who were looking forward to Blakey's epic walk. Not to be outdone, another repair was carried out, this time using a length of galvanised anchor-chain which looked somewhat out-of-place on a sophisticated multi-million-dollar yacht, but did the trick nonetheless.

With the boat breaking around us, we all became a little 'gun-shy' as we backed off slightly with the wind up to 50 knots. It is a fine line that we have to tread between pushing the boat recklessly and risking terminal damage and not pushing hard enough

Baz is not impressed with the situation as he brings the sewing machine on deck to repair the damaged mainsail.

Southern Ocean sleigh ride.

and losing ground to those who are prepared to take the risk. We had a buffer from the first leg; therefore, we sailed conservatively through the gales and, while we lost ground to the leaders, at least were still pretty much in one piece. While we had been suffering downtime it was nothing compared to some of the boats further back. To anyone listening in on that evening's sched, it must have sounded like a game of poker as Lowlife opened with a report of our damage. Murray Ross from Fishpie countered immediately with, 'I can top that, we pulled a spinnaker halyard winch clean out of the deck, jamming it against the mast'. Not to be outdone, Graeme Handley, the Kiwi navigator on *NCB Ireland* came in straight away with, 'Well I can beat that! We've broken our boom, spinnaker pole and blown out a spinnaker and headsail'.

With the decks covered in snow and ice, we reflected that these were conditions that Eskimos would have felt comfortable in — not yachtsmen! Jimmy Buffett hit the nail on the head when he wrote his song 'Changes in Latitudes, Changes in Attitudes'. A sail change which would be attacked with zest in the tropics is an altogether different proposition at 50° South. One particularly vicious squall in the middle of the night had everyone skating their way around the icy foredeck wrestling with the No. 2 jib top, trying to lower it to the deck as the wind increased to 50 knots accompanied by heavy snow. The angry Kevlar sail had other ideas and after wrestling with the damned thing for 15 minutes we finally got it down to the deck. Our hands were so numb it was almost impossible to run the zipper on the sail-bag.

The best thing about the cold and the snow was the snow fights on deck. Spike sculptured a snowman on the aft deck, complete with forks for arms and other necessary appendages styled out of tinfoil. It remained on deck for most of the day until someone got sick of it and smashed their boot into it — that summed up our mood during that week.

In these intensely cold conditions the four hours spent on standby were not a lot more pleasant than those spent on deck. It was necessary to be fully dressed, which meant being dressed in wet clothing. Unlike the on-watch who were keeping warm by moving around, the standby watch tried to sleep on the freezing sails in the companionway. After half an hour's lying on these sails, you would always wake up shivering. In an effort to alleviate this problem we used 'space blankets', which were plastic sheets with a foil lining. Whenever anyone was tucked up inside one of these sheets they took on the appearance of a roast chicken about to be put into the oven. One dark night, while sitting down aft beneath the hatch waiting for the red standby alarm light to be activated as the boat blasted down the seas on the edge of control, Spike asked, 'How far to the drop zone?' Apparently he felt like a paratrooper waiting to be dropped into enemy territory.

Eventually the gale abated as the low-pressure system sped off eastwards. Fortunately *F & P* up ahead of us was also into lighter air. As the atmosphere on board improved with both our position in the fleet and the weather improving, things were not going well on the 80-foot cruising division entrant, *Creightons Naturally*. During a violent broach, two crewmen were lost overboard; both were recovered but efforts

to revive Anthony Phillips failed and three days later he was buried at sea. News of Phillips's death was received on board our boat during the sched and brought home to us in the cruellest way that the sea does demand total respect. There was a distinctly subdued atmosphere aboard Big Red that day as each of us privately reflected on how tenuous our grip on life can be. Throughout this leg a total of five people fell overboard. All but one of them were retrieved alive from the freezing water.

After the drama of the gale, we were relieved with the change in the weather. Not so pleased were *Rothmans, Merit* and *F & P*. Over the next few days we pulled up alongside the sloops and caught up to within 40 miles of Dalts, who obviously had lighter winds ahead of us. The wild card was the Finnish maxi *Martela*, which was blasting in strong westerlies 52° 30′ South and, in fact, was in the lead. We were not too concerned, as at some stage soon they would have to try and get up to our latitude, which the weather maps indicated would not be easy for them.

By day twenty we were approaching the Kerguelen Islands, a French meteorological station. You would have to have done something pretty bad to be sent there for a tour of duty. These islands were ultimately to prove to be Fishpie's undoing. As we neared the islands, still accompanied by *Merit* and *Rothmans*, which

'If this repair breaks I'll walk home naked.'

were out of sight somewhere in the fog, the wind freshened once more and swung aft. *F & P,* further to the north of us, was forced to gybe onto port and sail around the north of the islands to avoid running into the 'real estate', as we called land. This gave us the chance to make some sort of a break on *F & P.* As we sailed beneath the Kerguelens a front passed and the breeze swung through to the northwest, allowing us to gybe onto port tack. As we gybed, sheets of ice broke away from the rig and sails and crashed onto the deck. It was about then we thought, 'Let's get the hell out of this place!'. It was amazing to see the change in attitude amongst the guys, just at the thought of heading north out of the Southern Ocean. After three weeks of cold, snow and ice we were more than ready for some warm sunshine.

Having rounded the Kerguelens we had a mere 2000 miles to sail to Fremantle. Most offshore yachtsmen consider the Sydney-Hobart a long race and here we were, getting all excited about *only* having three Sydney-Hobarts to go. The last week was always going to be difficult for Mike and Peter, trying to negotiate the large high-pressure system. As a basic rule of thumb, any area of high pressure means light winds, which of course slows our progress. The trick was to avoid the high for as long as possible. *F & P,* ever since rounding the Kerguelens, had been considerably further

Southern Ocean blues.

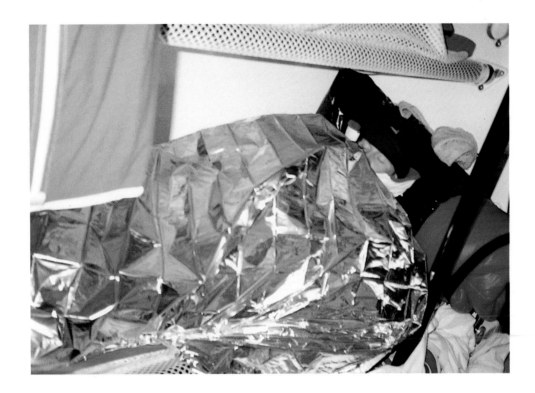

north than Big Red and the sloops. Our biggest concern at this stage was keeping a loose cover on *Merit,* which was only 11½ hours behind us at the beginning of the leg.

With 1150 miles to the finish, there were seven boats spread within 50 miles of the lead. One was the lightweight Spanish flyer, *Fortuna,* which earlier in the leg had smashed all records by sailing 402 miles in 24 hours. The final 1000 miles were sailed in predominantly light winds. Mike's analysis of the situation had agreed with the Apple computer's routing programme, which said we had to get north as fast as we could to break into a new band of breeze.

At the time we felt that *F & P* would beat us to the new breeze, but we pulled a big chunk out of her in the very light winds. We knew we were close when the log read, 'It's our God-given right to catch and pass Fishpie. We must be getting close, I can smell the used lolly wrappers from Raw Meat's [*F & P* watch captain] lolly jar'.

We were in for an incredibly tense last two days as we trimmed and steered the boat as if sailing the last leg of an America's Cup race. The twice-daily scheds became our lifeline to hear how we were going against the enemy. Our light-air performance was to be our winning edge as we wriggled our way into a five-mile

Baz attempts to keep warm under a space blanket.

lead over *F & P* and the sloops. With the leading boats approaching Rottnest Island from various angles, just over the horizon from each other, you could have cut the air on board Big Red with a knife. Finally we arrived off Rottnest, which we had to round before sailing the final 14 miles to the finish off Fremantle; it was pitch black with very flukey winds and we were incredibly nervous. 'Where is *F & P*? What about *Merit* and *Rothmans*? Are those their navigation lights off our beam? Come on guys, keep the boat moving and concentrate on the headsail trim.' We were like cats on a hot tin roof as we fought for every extra boatlength. The communication never ceased as we coaxed the last reserves of energy out of each other.

We crawled around Rottnest Island, still peering anxiously into the night looking for the enemy when suddenly we were bathed in light as spectator and media boats alike descended upon us. A flood of relief swept through the crew as we realised we were leading. Frowns broke into grins of delight and it was then we could enjoy the sight of land for the first time in 29 days, and mellow out for the sail to the finish across the racing waters of the 1987 America's Cup, in which four of our crew had competed aboard *KZ-7*.

The huge boom that emanated from the cannon on the finish-line confirmed our victory and signalled the end to what some of the crew described as the worst month of their lives. Certainly, it was a sweeter victory than the first leg, as we had to work so much harder for it. Having beaten *Rothmans* and *Merit*, who match-raced to the finish, by 93 minutes and *F & P* by three hours, we had done all we had hoped.

'I swear to God that flying fish was this long.'
Tired, but happy to have won the toughest leg.

Leg Two: Punta del Este — Fremantle (7650 miles)

Class	Boat Name		Elapsed Time			Finishing Position	Handicap Position	Overall Elapsed After 2 Legs
		Days	Hours	Mins	Secs			
A	Steinlager 2	27	5	34	44	1	1	1
A	Rothmans	27	7	7	28	2	3	4
A	Merit	27	7	7	56	3	2	2
A	Fisher & Paykel NZ	27	8	30	20	4	4	3
A	Charles Jourdan	27	22	16	41	5	5	9
A	The Card	27	22	57	57	6	6	5
A	Martela O.F.	28	1	27	57	7	8	6
A	Union Bank of Finland	28	5	13	52	8	9	11
A	Fortuna Extra Lights	28	5	52	22	9	7	7
A	Fazisi	29	1	40	15	10	10	8
A	Gatorade	29	5	39	14	11	11	10
A	British Defender	29	10	1	43	12	12	12
A	NCB Ireland	29	10	39	2	13	13	14
A	Belmont Finland II	29	15	57	55	14	14	13
C	Equity & Law II	31	22	28	36	15	15	15
A	Liverpool Enterprise	33	3	0	26	16	17	16
D	Maiden	35	11	11	41	17	16	17
D	Rucanor Sport	36	17	57	43	18	18	19
D	Schlussel Von Bremen	36	18	4	42	19	20	20
D	L'Esprit de Liberte	36	18	9	59	20	19	18
CRUISE	With Integrity	37	18	19	55	21	22	21
CRUISE	Creightons Naturally	40	9	45	43	22	23	22
D	La Poste	40	15	33	31	23	21	23

CHAPTER SEVEN

Homeward Bound

Recovering from what was, for many of us, the toughest month of our lives took at least a week once we had arrived in Fremantle. Our wives and girlfriends, who had flown across from Auckland to join us, were almost as tired, having had a sleepless night waiting to see who would be first across the line.

Not surprisingly the F & P crew were very disappointed with their fourth placing in the leg, having led for much of the way. We felt for them but were very happy all the same to have that win under our belts. Home for the *Steinlager* crew during our stay in 'Freo' was the Fremantle Hotel, where we also dined much of the time, enhancing the family atmosphere amongst everyone. The first few days were a junk-food frenzy as at last we were able to stroll down the street and indulge in the 'cop-the-lot' burgers and milkshakes that we used to fantasise about during the second leg as we sat down to a meal of freeze-dried food which by the end of the leg was about as appealing as a tin of Jellimeat.

A walk along the dock at the Fremantle Sailing Club, where the fleet was berthed, was all that was required to see just how hard the 7600-mile marathon through the Southern Ocean had been. The scene was more like that of a demolition derby pit than a dock, with broken rigging and torn sails strewn everywhere as the crews worked to get their boats back into racing condition again. We pulled our rigs out of the boat and Tim Gurr, Roy Mason and Don Walker from Southern Pacific Boatyard flew across from Auckland to rebuild the titanium spinnaker halyard crane, which had been badly cracked during the leg.

After the hassles of Punta del Este, where we could not communicate with the locals or even read the menus in the restaurants, it was a pleasure to be back in a society similar to our own, where we could get things done on the boat with a minimum of fuss and eat food we were familiar with.

Once we had finished our maintenance schedule on the boat, having replaced anything at all suspect and been out sailing to check the new sails for the next leg, we had a few days off to unwind and go on holiday. Most of us hired cars and drove down to the wine-producing region of Margaret River. With many of the crews holidaying in the same area we saw almost as much of each other around the countryside and vineyards as we did in Fremantle.

Throughout our stay in Freo, Trae continued to bang on our doors every morning at 6.45 to get everyone out for an hour of fitness training. Most mornings we would run to a nearby park where we would be put through a series of circuit exercises. By far the most popular form of training was a game of touch rugby amongst ourselves. Unfortunately, Blakey was very 'anti' us playing footie, because of the risk of someone getting injured and not being able to sail the next leg. Therefore, whenever we talked

With the squall past, Big Red powers up the Waitemata and we can finally start to enjoy the atmosphere.

about playing a game of rugby, we would refer to it in code as playing 'touch cricket'. On many occasions we drew blank stares from people overhearing our conversation and wondering what the hell we were talking about.

One morning we were all in the park, lined up in teams facing each other with rugby ball in hand ready to begin the game. Exactly at that time, who should happen to come running across the park towards us, but Blakey on his morning run. The scene that followed was like something out of a Keystone Cops movie as we threw the ball at each other like a hot potato, not wanting to be caught with the evidence, while some of us dropped to the ground in spontaneous bursts of press-ups. Peter just continued running by with a wry smile on his face. There is nothing worse than being caught with your hand in the cookie jar.

Someone in the Whitbread race organisation had a warped sense of humour when they made the decision to start the third leg two days before Christmas. As we tapered off on our drinking habits in the week before the start, to make sure our bodies were not total wrecks when we left port, we decided to have our own

After a month at sea, the first few days in port were a junk-food frenzy. Billy tucks into a 'cop the lot' burger.

Christmas party at our hotel. In addition to the crew and our wives and girlfriends, we had the company of Peter Montgomery and his wife Claudia. I don't think either of them could quite believe their eyes as the crew performed like trained seals, no doubt fuelled by the magnum of champagne we had won on leg two.

The catering for the dinner was a drama in itself, as the restaurant manager bought a large pig to be served. Unfortunately, you cannot put an apple in a pig's mouth when it has no head. So off she went in search of a head, eventually returning with the necessary piece of anatomy. To her frustration, she realised that the pig had no ears, so she set off once more in pursuit of two ears. Returning a couple of hours later with the ears, she presented them to the chef to sew on. The final straw came when the chef informed her that they were both left ears.

On the eve of the race start we had our usual pre-race briefing amongst the crew. Peter did not have to tell us the importance of the forthcoming leg to Auckland. If there was one leg of the race that we wanted to win, this was the one. No Kiwi yacht had ever been first into Auckland before and we were all fired up to make sure Big Red led the fleet into the Waitemata Harbour and across the finish-line.

Both Kiwi ketches left Freo with one thought in their minds – to be first into Auckland.

However, we had no illusions as we knew that Dalts and his crew on *F & P* would be very hungry for a win, especially after the disappointment of the second leg.

Mike showed us, on the charts, the course and the likely route we would take along the way. He had been regularly to the Perth weather office and had the latest predictions, which were explained at length so that everyone on board knew exactly what to expect. Some of the other boats perhaps did not understand the importance of a solid game-plan. It was equally important that the navigator be flexible, as the strategy needs constant updating throughout the leg as new weather information is received.

The morning of the start produced the first rainfall we had seen since we had arrived in Fremantle. The good news was that this was accompanied by a fresh westerly air flow in place of the usual southwesterly sea breeze which the locals refer to as the 'Fremantle Doctor'. This meant that instead of a beat into the wind leaving Freo, we would be on a very fast reach with the wind from abeam.

Milling around before the start, prior to hoisting our sails, we could not help but smile at Pierre Fehlmann, standing at the helm of *Merit* dressed in his bright yellow wet-weather gear as the rain pelted down, nonchalantly puffing away on a huge cigar,

'Come on guys, there's a whole ocean out here. Do we have to sail this close to each other?'

oblivious of his surroundings. To make the most of the start for the spectators, the local Whitbread officials sent us first to a turning mark off beautiful Cottesloe Beach, followed by an eight-mile beat out around Rottnest Island, before reaching southwards.

Fehlmann, obviously benefiting from his cigar, got the best of the start to lead Big Red around the first mark, with Fishpie snapping hard on our heels. On the beat out across Gage Roads to Rottnest, Brad called into play some of the 'Kiwi Magic' he learnt racing in these waters on *KZ-7*, to see us picking some good shifts to be right on *Merit*'s tail for the turn south, with *F & P* and *Rothmans* 300 metres astern.

The wind increased to 35 knots which, combined with the big seaway running, gave us an abrupt reminder that we were back into it again. *Merit* was proving to be difficult to overhaul in these conditions and we remained abeam of the Swiss boys until dusk, when they speared off to leeward of us into the darkness. Throughout the night we monitored *F & P* and *Rothmans* astern of us on the radar. *F & P* was easy to keep track of as she remained exactly 200 metres astern, which had us looking over our shoulders the whole time to see her navigation lights, looking like a pair of red and green eyes following us. During the night Peter and Mike had a few anxious moments as we negotiated Cape Naturalist and its associated reefs. In total darkness

For 3500 miles the 'white shark' was our constant companion.

and the breaking seas glowing white, it was very hard to see exactly where we were, so the radar and Satnav were glowing red hot from constant use.

Dawn on day two revealed *Merit* in front and to leeward, while *F & P* was still behind us. The wind strength was right up and, if anything, the seas had built even more, which was making for some extremely fast sailing. Undoubtedly reaching in these conditions is the wettest point of sail. A feature of Farr's Whitbread designs is the flared bow which prevents the boat from nose-diving excessively. Another result of the flared bow is that the bow wave is tossed up and away from the hull, which means that large volumes of water can be blown across the flush deck, resulting in a crew that closely resemble drowned rats. To come on deck without full wet-weather gear, as Mike did on occasions for a quick smoke, is about as sensible as walking through a car wash in a business suit.

The bumpy conditions made for a distinctly subdued atmosphere on board as we all slowly developed our sea-legs once more. Therefore, there was not quite the same enthusiasm at meal-times. Because of the amount of water coming across the deck, it was necessary to keep all of the hatches shut, with the result that the interior of the boat became very stuffy. BC, who never failed to produce a meal whatever

Christmas Day was business as usual on board.

the circumstances, was finding the conditions particularly unpleasant. As he stood in the heaving galley stirring the stew, he had his head down the sink throwing up at the same time. There was much conjecture, judging by the appearance of the stew, as to whether he made it to the sink!

Throughout the morning we were to play a game of cat-and-mouse with *F & P*, as she would attack and we defended. The roles were reversed on a couple of occasions as we exchanged the lead. *F & P* first broke through on a spectacular surf no more than 50 metres to windward of us. In the pale light we could see Keith Chapman helming Fishpie as he finally hooked onto the right wave. The sight of a maxi with five sails set surfing down the face of the grey seas at over 20 knots with water being thrown everywhere was unforgettable.

Shoebie was on the helm of Big Red and did not enjoy being passed by the enemy on the white boat. With both the standby and regular watches on deck we counter-attacked, searching for every wave that would gain us back precious metres. Again and again we scorched down the seas with the spray flying everywhere, almost reducing visibility to nil as we surfed up to within a couple of metres before being forced to bear away to leeward of *F & P*. We were trimming all five sails constantly as we tried relentlessly to break through. We eventually found the elusive wave and in a blast of spray we gave the white boat her own medicine back as we blasted over the top of her and into the lead. *Merit* and *Rothmans* were unable to hold the duelling Kiwis and by the end of the day they had both disappeared over the horizon behind us. It was becoming apparent that we had one hell of a fight on our hands for the 3400-mile 'sprint' home.

Christmas Day arrived and was something of a non-event on board Big Red. We thought of our families back home sitting down and tucking into the roast turkey and leg of ham. In a continuation of our weight-saving policy we had no fresh food 'treats' or champagne on board, as most of the other boats had, to celebrate the day. We even went to the extremes that no Christmas presents were allowed on board as they were too heavy, so we had opened all of our presents in Fremantle before starting the leg. We were highly amused later to see video footage off some of the other boats who had celebrated Christmas with all the trimmings. Our Christmas dinner was the usual freeze-dried gastronomic delight; on this occasion it was curry and rice with a dessert of hot custard and sponge cake.

The conditions were still bumpy and we were making very good progress across the Great Australian Bight when the highlight of Christmas Day occurred. *Fortuna*, which was obviously enjoying the strong winds, had sailed over the horizon from behind with a spinnaker set, and was a mile off our leeward beam when she wiped out in spectacular fashion. She got knocked down so far that it was a case of 'now you see me, now you don't'.

We were beginning to wonder if the wind was ever going to ease away when after five days we were still experiencing a very fast, albeit wet, ride. Mike was forever being asked when the wind was going to moderate as weather maps with conflicting scenarios were fed out of the weather fax. On the fifth night we just about smashed

into *F & P*'s stern, as our paths converged once more. Ross was on the helm as we scorched down a large wave with the deck enveloped in spray, giving us very little visibility, when *F & P*'s illuminated transom suddenly appeared no more than a few metres in front of our bow. As we sliced across her transom with our hearts in our mouths, we decided that it was an awfully big ocean and it was not entirely necessary to be right on top of *F & P* the whole time, so we separated by a couple of miles.

It was something of a relief when the wind did finally moderate on day six, as we were all beginning to resemble gorillas with our arms stretched longer from the incessant strain of steering the boat when it was fully powered up. On numerous occasions, we had needed a 'shot-gun' helmsman to stand by the leeward wheel ready to help pull on the wheel if the helmsman could not manage on his own.

During the extended period of strong winds, Alain Gabbay's *Charles Jourdan* had blasted into the lead. Her moment of glory was short-lived as both *F & P* and Big Red overhauled her in the light winds that followed as we approached Tasmania. *F & P*'s navigator Murray Ross had called a few good shots and the white boat led us around Tasmania and into the Tasman Sea by seven miles. With *F & P* just on the horizon in front of us, Brad decided it was time to 'point the bone' at her. Whenever Brad did this it was usually the kiss of death to the recipient of his curse. This occasion was to be no different.

Blasting across the bottom of Australia. The mizzen staysail was a real work-horse in these conditions.

Perfect cruising conditions but . . .

Rothmans was still a threat to us, 25 miles astern, while Merit with a damaged steering system was a comfortable 85 miles behind. Our confidence was soon eroded as we were becalmed off the ironically named Storm Bay on the east coast of Tasmania. Merit picked up 60 miles on us as we sat in sight of F & P, going nowhere and rapidly losing our sense of humour. The breeze began to filter in again from astern as squalls developed behind us. Our biggest concern now was to make sure that Fishpie did not wriggle away from us during the night.

New Year's Eve arrived and was celebrated with the same lack of enthusiasm as Christmas Day. It did not seem natural to be sitting becalmed with no wind, worrying about where the opposition were, when all of our friends were partying hard ashore. Trae decided that if he could not have a drink, then he would at least pretend he was having a high old time. At the midnight change of watch he stumbled out through the main hatch, tripped over winches and sheets, and slurring his words, stated that 'thish ish the best New Year'sh Eve I've had in-hic-agesh'.

The first sched of the New Year was listened to with more than the usual interest. Whenever we had a slow 12-hour run in light winds, the next sched would be listened to with a degree of apprehension. Did the other boats have similar conditions or had they 'jagged one' and got away from us? To our relief we had, in fact, gone extremely well overnight to pull 14 miles out of the white boat and move into a seven-mile lead. With 800 miles to Cape Reinga and a large high-pressure system giving

Shoebie steers, Blakey looks for breeze, while Ross checks out the 'white shark'.

Big Red makes painfully slow progress up the Tasman. This shot was taken from an RNZAF Orion.

Blakey searching for breeze as we reach across the top of the North Island. Twenty years of experience combined with his lucky socks made him unbeatable.

light winds to the whole Tasman Sea, we were going to be in for a tense time until the finish.

Our match-race with *F & P* continued the whole way to Cape Reinga in very light conditions. It was a constant see-sawing effect as first she would carry the breeze up to us and then we would wriggle away again. We were forced to show *F & P* our winning technique in light winds as we attempted to hold her at bay. Instead of trying to carry a spinnaker downwind in light airs, we had discovered while training in Auckland before the race that we were much faster sailing downwind with a light genoa set, keeping the apparent wind forward on the boat. This was a technique that Peter and Mike had learned on the trimaran and had won us the leg into Fremantle.

One hundred miles out from Cape Reinga we had *F & P* tucked away three miles astern as we monitored her constantly on the radar. There was a startled yell from Marko as he saw a blip racing across the screen. We could not figure out what it was until we looked up and saw a RNZAF Orion flying over the top of us. At least it wasn't *F & P* switching into hyper-drive. Our biggest concern was now *Rothmans,* which was right in on the Northland coast and in a position to sail around us if the wind swung in direction. That was all we needed — a wild card as well as *F & P* to worry about.

Approaching Cape Reinga early in the morning of day 13 there was great excitement on board. We had our first glimpse of Godzone since we had flown to England six months earlier. Apparently the boys on *F & P* were just as fired up about coming home as they caught up to within 200 metres of us before we caught a wind shift and stretched back out to a three-mile lead. As we rounded Cape Reinga we got a taste of what was to come. Local fishermen were out in force and the cape itself looked like a grandstand with hundreds of people watching the epic match-race between their two Kiwi boats. 'Huey' had smiled on us and the wind had remained constant to put *Rothmans* ten miles astern. They now had their own private battle with a much-improved *Merit.*

Sailing across the top of New Zealand to North Cape the watch system was cancelled. Auckland was only 200 miles away and it was going to take a lot of work on our part to make sure we were first home. There would be plenty of time for sleeping after we had won this leg. Once around North Cape we had the wind behind us for the sprint down the Northland coast. As night closed in, our eyes were constantly on *F & P;* the last thing we could afford to do was let her separate from us. Approaching Cape Brett, the wind began to freshen just as *F & P* did a Houdini disappearing routine by turning off the navigation lights. A sharp call over the VHF radio telling them their lights were off had the desired effect and we spotted her again, although she had gybed away from us towards the shore while we couldn't see her.

Throughout the night we defended our lead jealously, as gybe after gybe we covered their every move. By dawn the adrenalin level was reaching maximum amongst the crew as we sailed past Whangarei Heads and an early morning reception committee. At this time Blakey took the helm, where he was to stay until the finish

Watches and meals were cancelled as we match-raced Fisher & Paykel down the Northland coast.

with Brad calling the tactics, while the trimmers concentrated on extracting every ounce of speed out of Big Red.

We held *F & P* one mile astern as we blasted past Flat Rock off Kawau Island. The number of boats out to meet us was incredible and spurred us on as *F & P* carried a freshening breeze down to close the gap. The atmosphere on board was totally electric as we willed the finish-line closer. The sky over Auckland was starting to look ominous, so Mike went down to the nav station to listen to the radio for any updated weather reports. At that moment a listener had called Newstalk 1ZB from Titirangi, saying a southerly front had just passed through. That was all it took for Blakey to order a small genoa to be made ready and for everyone to be ready to drop the spinnaker at a moment's notice.

Meanwhile, 20 miles astern the two cigarette boats had their own battle past Sail Rock.

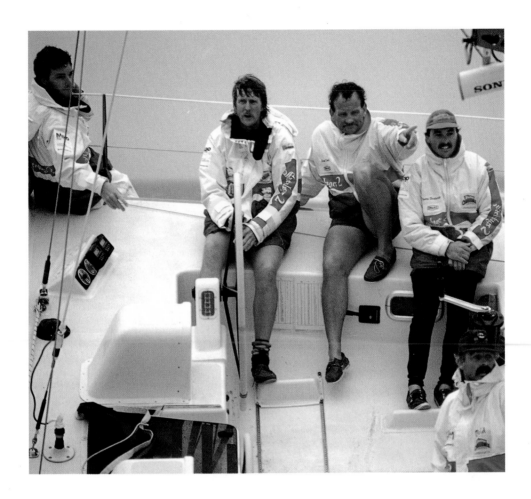

Peter's 20 years of ocean-racing experience paid huge dividends in one dramatic minute as he screamed *'Get rid of it!'*, the instant we saw the wind change on the water a mile in front of us. We worked like men possessed to drop the spinnaker and mizzen staysail before the squall hit. Dalts and his boys, trying desperately to catch us, were not as prepared and were caught with their spinnaker still up and were soon in big trouble. It was impossible not to detect a strong note of satisfaction in Blakey's voice as he said 'Got the bastards'.

With the initial fury of the squall past and our one-mile lead over *F & P* restored, we were able to enjoy the sail from Whangaparaoa along the East Coast Bays to the finish. The rookies on board who hadn't sailed a Whitbread before could not believe the spectacle that was unfolding in front of us as boats of every shape and size came

Blakey and the three watch captains: Ross, Shoebie and Brad. Blood spilt on deck during the squall is still evident on the cockpit floor.

All hands on deck as we weave our way through the spectator craft to the finish-line.

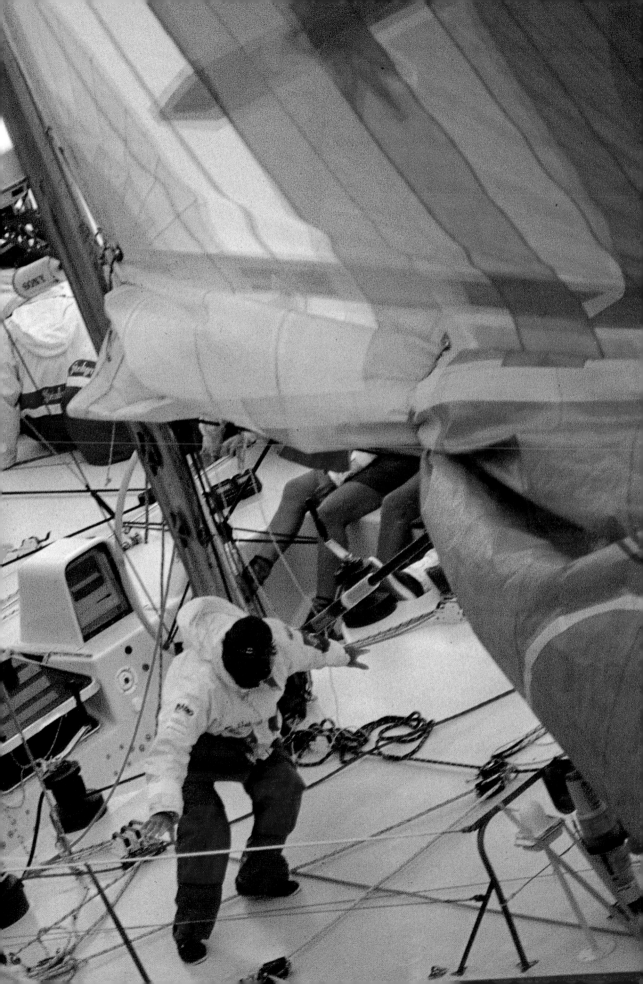

out to welcome us home. Even those of us who had experienced an Auckland Whitbread finish, could not believe the incredible enthusiasm of the thousands of Kiwis who had braved the shocking weather to watch Big Red make history.

It was fortunate that it was raining as we sailed up the harbour as it helped to disguise the damp eyes amongst the crew. The emotions we experienced crossing the finish-line off Orakei Wharf were impossible to describe. Turning the corner into the arrival berth at Princes Wharf was overwhelming and we were stunned by the reception that these people were giving us. Amidst the cheers and clapping of the crowd was a fantastic big red boat with 15 very proud Kiwis lining her deck. We were home!

David Fletcher's viewpoint in the NZ Herald.

Our wives and girlfriends were our greatest supporters: they felt the tension, as we approached the finish-line, and the joy, when we celebrated at Princes Wharf.

Leg Three: Fremantle — Auckland (3434 miles)

Class	Boat Name	Days	Elapsed Time Hours	Mins	Secs	Finishing Position	Handicap Position	Overall Elapsed After 3 Legs
A	Steinlager 2	12	17	33	0	1	1	1
A	Fisher & Paykel NZ	12	17	39	4	2	2	3
A	Merit	12	18	44	17	3	3	2
A	Rothmans	12	18	54	37	4	5	4
A	The Card	12	20	49	50	5	6	5
A	Fortuna Extra Lights	12	21	22	22	6	4	8
A	Martela O.F.	12	22	42	57	7	7	6
A	British Defender	12	23	29	25	8	8	9
A	Charles Jourdan	13	2	53	49	9	9	7
A	Fazisi	13	4	40	30	10	10	10
A	Gatorade	13	5	11	8	11	11	11
A	NCB Ireland	13	10	50	24	12	12	13
A	Belmont Finland II	13	14	27	42	13	15	12
A	Liverpool Enterprise	14	14	17	58	14	19	16
C	Equity & Law II	14	16	55	13	15	17	15
A	Union Bank of Finland	14	20	40	6	16	21	14
CRUISE	With Integrity	14	22	50	2	17	20	21
CRUISE	Creightons Naturally	15	4	12	4	18	22	22
D	Maiden	15	5	27	14	19	13	17
D	L'Esprit de Liberte	15	6	17	16	20	14	18
D	Schlussel Von Bremen	15	8	21	58	21	16	20
D	Rucanor Sport	15	23	31	41	22	18	19
D	La Poste	18	23	18	23	23	23	23

CHAPTER EIGHT

Back Into The Chilli Bin

Having spent two weeks in a race that was as demanding physically as it was mentally, it took us some time to come back down to earth. The afternoon of our arrival saw dozens of family and friends on board *Steinlager 2* for some serious partying. Peter Andrews, the importer of Moët champagne, delivered a case of his product which really helped to stir things along.

Because of the relative shortness of the leg and the light winds holding the leaders up in the Tasman Sea, the fleet finished over a comparatively short period of time. The Auckland stopover has always been the most popular amongst the Whitbread crews because of the fantastic welcome each boat receives. It was great to see that the New Zealand public lived up to their reputation and turned out at Princes Wharf at all hours of the day and night to applaud the crews as they arrived.

In comparison to the other stopovers throughout the race, Auckland was always going to be the most hectic for the *Steinlager* crew. Because of the relative ease in carrying out maintenance at home, we had waited until Auckland to give the boat a major refit. Few of our competitors could believe the good condition of Big Red's hull when we hauled her out of the water at the Devonport naval base. This was the first time the boat had been out of the water since it had been lifted off the ship in Zeebrugge six months earlier. At last Lawrie Smith had his chance to have a look at Big Red's 'cheating' hull out of the water.

While the boat was having its bottom repainted we had both rigs in at the Southern Spars factory for a very thorough check. All fittings were dye-tested for cracks and fatigue. With no major problems the rigs were given a clean bill of health and re-stepped into the boat once it went back into the water. Most of the fleet were hauled out during the stopover to comply with the race rules which stipulate that rigs and rudders be removed for a check-up.

The overseas crews took advantage of their break to go sightseeing around the countryside and all were impressed with the scenery and hospitality they experienced. While the other crews were away touring, we found ourselves incredibly busy with the boat refit and the opportunity to catch up with family and friends. It was almost impossible to get away from the boat, as interest was so intense we were forever showing people around. After the relative tranquillity of two weeks at sea the atmosphere of Princes Wharf was at times a little overwhelming. On occasions, we were all guilty of not being overly effervescent and chatty, but with the race only halfway through it weighed heavily on our minds that we still had a long way to go and a lot of work to do.

One of the highlights of the stay in Auckland was the ticker-tape parade up Queen Street which saw every crew on a float up to a civic reception at the Town Hall. The *Merit* guys apparently decided that it was too hot and that everyone needed

Goddy and Deano in 'Frontierland'.

cooling down and embarked on a water-bomb attack of the other floats. Having been caught without any ammunition during a similar parade in Fremantle, we were ready for action this time, armed to the teeth with a box full of water bombs. As we slowly made our way up Queen Street amidst the streamers and cheering crowds, skirmishes flared up between the crews and on occasions unsuspecting members of the public were caught in the crossfire. Peter Montgomery, standing on the side of the road, became an instant target and only some deft footwork saved him from a soaking. By the time we got to the Town Hall we all looked as if we had been at sea for a week.

During the third leg we were told on the radio that we had been named, as a crew, New Zealand Yachtsman of the Year. Our award was presented to us at a ceremony beside the boat by the Governor-General, Sir Paul Reeves. Having been given this award we really felt that we had to carry on and win the race or we would look a bit silly.

This wasn't the only formal function we attended in Auckland. There was already a preponderance of married guys aboard Big Red and two more took the fall in Auckland — Shoebie to Sally Sharp and Deano to Tracy Taylor. Not only did Sally and Tracy have to organise their own weddings, they only had a couple of weeks

Sailing out of the Waitemata Harbour was a little like sailing up a river in flood.

with their new husbands before they put to sea once more. Their married lives could only get better.

An interesting comparison of differing approaches to leadership could be seen when the nearby bungi jumping attracted the attention of many of the crews. In keeping with Blakey's 'no accidents' policy we were told in no uncertain terms that we were not allowed to jump. In contrast, one English skipper allegedly told his crew that if they did not jump they were 'chickens'. Many of his crew were veterans of the last Whitbread aboard *Drum* and *Atlantic Privateer* where they had earned the reputation of being hard players both ashore and at sea, so a bungi jump was probably just a stroll in the park for them anyway.

At our pre-race crew briefing we had our usual weather report from Mike, but Peter had also invited Jim Blair along to give us a pep-talk. Having had three straight wins, Peter was taking no chances of letting complacency set in and after Jim's talk we left the room with renewed enthusiasm, intent on continuing the trend and taking out the Grand Slam by winning all six legs.

The morning of the start of leg four, back into the Southern Ocean around Cape Horn and up to Punta del Este once more, arrived with the crew of Big Red ready

'It's hard to think of a more demoralising way to start a leg . . .'

to get back into it. There are always mixed feelings when leaving our families again, but after a hectic month ashore we were keen to get on with the business at hand. With the highly successful Commonwealth Games finishing in Auckland on the previous day, all attention was turned to the spectacle of the re-start. The crowds of cheering Kiwis lining Princes Wharf soon had our adrenalin level pumped up again as we motored through the thousands of spectator boats to the start area off North Head. The RNZAF Kiwi Red aerobatic team did their stuff overhead and set the scene for the day. Our start was unmemorable as we got stuck back from the line in light airs, but with 6255 miles remaining we were not overly concerned. The start must have been a bad dream for Swede Magnus Olson, as he steered *The Card* through the moored spectator craft, catching the mizzen mast on the rigging of a spectator boat resulting in a very spectacular mizzen dismasting for *The Card*. On board *Steinlager 2* we could hardly believe our eyes and there was a chorus of 'Oh, the poor buggers!'. It was hard to think of a more demoralising way to start the leg.

Finding the first turning mark off the East Coast Bays amongst the solid wall of spectator boats was an interesting experience. Once around, the moored boats looked impenetrable and Blakey was wearing a path between the two steering wheels as he ran from one side of the boat to the other trying to get a decent view of

A good ten miles after the start and we've still got half of Auckland with us.

proceedings. As Peter was ducking and weaving through the boats, Mike had his own minor panic as he realised he still had his wife Robi's car and house keys in his pocket which he had forgotten to give her in the heat of the moment when we left the dock. A quick phone call over the VHF radio established that Robi had a spare set of keys, so Mike could stop cursing and start concentrating once more.

The waters around Cape Colville and Channel Island have a reputation for being rough, but this was certainly not the case this time as we sat totally becalmed in the company of the other leaders. The ultimate ignominy occurred when a guy in his dinghy rowed around us having a chat as we sat there going nowhere. *The Card* must have been beginning to wonder if they should have been a sloop all along as they picked up a breeze and sailed right around the outside of us and into the lead.

The atmosphere on board was subdued as we ate dinner down below that first night and thought of the families and friends we had waved goodbye to earlier in the day. Our families had accompanied us out for 30 miles on the *Sea Flight* before turning for home. At about that time Peter Montgomery, who had been broadcasting live from on board during the start, took his leave and much to the delight of the guys departed with a somewhat undignified leap over the side to be picked up by a waiting boat. Just another day in the life of a sports broadcaster.

In pleasant contrast to the start of the last two legs, we had a few days of light-airs sailing as we headed across the Bay of Plenty and around East Cape before heading away to the southeast towards the Chatham Islands. Everyone took advantage of the quiet conditions to catch up on some much-needed sleep after our busy month at home.

By day four, the regular pecking order had developed once more with *Merit*, *F & P*, *Steinlager 2* and *Rothmans* taking up the running at the head of the fleet. It must have been demoralising for the other maxis to see the same four boats out in front time after time. Shoebie was not unhappy on this day: he got to celebrate his birthday twice as we sailed across the international dateline. There was much conjecture as to whether that actually made him two years older. Less happy was Spike, who had the misfortune to have drawn head-cleaning duty and had the dubious privilege of scrubbing the toilet two days in a row.

Having worn shorts and T-shirts in the warm conditions of the first four days, we got a sharp reminder that this was a Southern Ocean leg after all as the wind swung through to the southwest and strengthened to give us conditions similar to those we experienced blasting across the bottom of Australia. *F & P* was only three miles off our beam, while *Merit* enjoyed a stint in the lead four miles ahead of us. Lawrie's boys on *Rothmans* had come unstuck in the light airs and were 30 miles astern. The prospect of close-reaching through the Southern Ocean held limited appeal; no-one enjoys being constantly lashed with near-freezing water.

The following afternoon with *F & P* still off our beam to windward the Dukes were on watch. Ross called for a headsail change from the No. 2 jib top to the No. 3 jib top as the wind increased to 35 knots. Six of the crew including Blakey ventured onto the foredeck to change the headsails. At the moment the headsail was being

dropped and gathered up a large wave caught the stern and threw the boat into a violent broach. Trae and Peter went for an impromptu swim but were fortunately both clipped on with their safety harnesses. Chaos reigned for a couple of minutes as bedraggled crewmen got back to their feet and heaved the headsail back on board. One of the recipients of a dunking suggested in the log that 'Ross prefers the leeward wheel for a better overall picture of the sea conditions', after Ross had been thrown off the windward steering wheel during the broach.

Eventually the wind swung aft and freshened even more, occasionally getting up to 45 knots to give us a helter-skelter ride for 12 hours. On one particularly rapid transit down a huge wave Blakey was on the helm having a great time as the speedo jumped up to 25 knots. The tricky bit came when it was time to avoid running into the bottom of the wave. It soon became apparent that there was no easy way out of it and we ploughed straight through the wave in front of us. For a few seconds Big Red was totally submerged as a wave of icy cold water cascaded back across the deck, enveloping everyone and slamming them against winches. The force of the wave was such that it knocked Peter's feet out from underneath him, leaving him trailing off the steering wheel hanging on with both hands. The rogue wave carried on over the stern of the boat washing all of our safety equipment overboard including our two life-rings and Danbuoy. After the initial shock of the freezing water we all looked at each other with inane grins as the cockpit took on the appearance of a paddling pool. Looking out through the hatches from inside the boat you almost expected to see a fish swim by amongst the ropes and sea-boots in the cockpit. The

Fazisi's navigator had circumnavigated the world underwater in a nuclear submarine. Fazisi's crew seemed destined to do the same.

noon position was entered in the log a short time later as 'underwater'. In these conditions we always made sure our safety harnesses were clipped on. We soon found out that torches and cameras had to be clipped on also, or they would be washed overboard.

Thinking we were in for an extended period of heavy-running conditions, we were just getting our teeth into it when the wind began to moderate and we soon found ourselves sailing at a slightly more sedate pace. Our course continued to take us to the south, where we levelled out at around 53° latitude. The temperature, while still very cold, was not the same as the intensely bitter cold we had experienced on leg two. However, it was still cold enough for Ross to have trouble with his feet and he soon developed a phenomenon known as 'Rossbite', otherwise referred to in more extreme cases as frostbite. In these freezing conditions everyone suffered from cold, numb feet and in a desperate effort to keep them warm, we cut up some of our foil 'space blankets' and wrapped them around our feet before putting our boots on. Ross was so intent on keeping his feet warm that he held his rubber sea-boots inverted over the stove to try and dry them. All he succeeded in doing was stinking the galley out with the stench of burning rubber.

The fact that we were in the Southern Ocean in summer meant that the pack ice was down beneath 60° South, although this did not mean that we saw fewer icebergs. By day nine we spotted our first iceberg of this leg; it was clearly visible at ten miles so it must have been huge. Long daylight hours made life a little less tense as the potential for hitting wayward 'growlers' — small broken-off bits of icebergs

The Kiwi Reds — Billy, Trae, Deano and Clutch — resplendent in their red balaclavas, knitted by Deano's grandmother.

— became proportionally less. Brad's watch, known up until now as the 'Foodtown watch' because of their propensity for stealing the other watches' chocolate allowance, were renamed this day as they appeared on deck resplendent in bright red balaclavas knitted by Deano's grandmother. They called themselves the 'Kiwi Reds' after the RNZAF Skyhawk pilots, whereas the rest of us felt that perhaps the 'Red Bonnet Brigade' was more appropriate.

A feature of our close racing against *F & P* was that we were within VHF radio range for much of the time and were able to chat to each other with no-one else being able to hear. Brad was speaking to Dalts on one such occasion and mentioned to him that we were racing on this leg with an extra crew member. After a period of stunned silence on board *F & P*, Brad told them who our 'extra' was. While in Auckland, Peter was approached by the family of an old Cape Horner, Frederick Thomas Chapman, who had recently passed away. Chapman sailed around the Horn on the barquentine *Garthneill* in 1924 and his family thought it fitting that we scatter his ashes as we rounded the Horn. Soon enough he came to be known as 'Dusty' Chapman and was considered by all of us to be a member of the crew. We were sure he enjoyed his last voyage to Cape Horn.

Back into the depths of the Southern Ocean and it was snow-time again. Any serious skier would have been in ecstasy at the sight of such perfect, dry-powder snow, yet it still seemed a little out of place on the deck of Big Red. Grim decided to liven up his day by forming a supply of snowballs and lobbing them down the main hatch into the galley. He was a little disconcerted when BC retaliated by throwing

Sailing in dry snow was an infinitely more pleasant proposition than wet drizzle. Spike trims, Foxy steers and Ross hides behind the mizzen.

some of our precious eggs back at him. We were soon to discover that eggs and dry snow are not a good combination.

Goddy was unanimously voted 'Dick of the Day' when he decided that it was too difficult to make up the powdered milk whenever we had hot drinks. To remedy this he decided to mix some milk powder into the tin of Milo. The problem occurred when he got the proportions wrong and the end result was a cup of brown hot milk. Having ruined our last tin of Milo, he was definitely not flavour of the day. It does not take much of a faux pas to incur the wrath of the crew.

F & P was still breathing down our neck, as by day ten we were five miles ahead of her. But not for long, however, as the next day we had the better of the breeze and were 52 miles further east than the white boat, while she was further south. With 2000 miles still to go to the Horn it was going to be a case of who got the weather systems right. A slow-moving trough of low pressure soon thwarted our progress as the wind swung forward to put us on the wind. Even with a bright, sunny day the

Heavy snow on the mizzen spinnaker.

There are some big chunks of real estate floating around the Southern Ocean.

icy wind chilled us to the bone as we slid past numerous icebergs glowing a translucent teal-coloured hue.

Sitting on deck in the middle of a foggy night in the dark, cold conditions it was the thought of all those supporters back home that helped us give that extra little bit and perhaps concentrate harder. Memories of our visit to Nelson during our publicity tour around New Zealand where we showed a terminally ill teenage girl over the boat are hard to forget. We got a letter from the girl's father in England before the race telling us that she had recently passed away and that their visit to *Steinlager 2* had been a big thrill for her. There were a lot of choked throats among the crew as we each read the letter and realised that Big Red meant a lot to many people.

In addition to our performance on the inter-yachts scheds, the other test of crew morale was the quality of the food. The closest thing to torture was to be on watch before breakfast-time and to smell BC's pancakes on the griddle wafting out through the hatch. The watches already eating breakfast often made a play of eating their pancakes and porridge in full view of the guys on deck. With a strict limit of two pancakes each, the on-coming watch often came on deck feigning indigestion and claiming they'd just eaten the on-watch's pancakes too. Another big hit with the crew was the bread BC baked in his pressure cooker during some mornings to be eaten at lunch-time, along with freeze-dried fish cakes, pasta or similar. Blakey's pet hate was pasta, so he occasionally had to settle for a cup of packet soup while the rest of us tucked into our macaroni or spaghetti. To keep our energy up in the cold conditions, BC would make a hot dessert with custard for afternoon tea. Four hours later at the 2000-hour change of watch we would eat dinner, which was any one of numerous freeze-dried delights. It is fortunate that BC is easy going as most people would have gone nuts being asked 14 times, 'What's for dinner tonight, BC?' Usually the evening meal consisted of a meat dish, potatoes, beans or peas, and another hot dessert — the most popular dessert being apple crumble and custard. The various freeze-dried meat dishes were known alternatively as Lamb From Out Of Town (Lamb Provençale) and Beef Strokemeoff (Beef Stroganoff), and the curry dishes were always referred to as Dodgy Vindaloos. Another speciality was Beef Sebago, named for its shoe-like texture. By the time we had finished each leg we'd had enough of tasteless meat and were fast becoming vegetarians and eating only the freeze-dried vegetables and desserts.

Approaching Cape Horn on our nineteenth night at sea we held a comfortable lead of 20 miles over the 'white shark', while *Merit* and *Rothmans* were safely tucked away over 100 miles astern. 'Huey' was obviously watching over us and had decided that we'd been having it too easy so far, and so we were confronted with very light, variable winds accompanied by heavy drizzle. Occasionally our radar lacked power and sometimes we treated it with scepticism, and with scathing sarcasm we referred to it as a 'stealth' radar. A stealth aircraft is undetectable, whereas our radar was unable to detect anything. As we got closer to the Horn we detected an uncharacteristically strong 'blip' on the screen five miles astern of us. The signal looked far too strong to be *F & P* so we assumed it was a large fishing-boat. At dawn we were shocked

to see that the radar had actually been working well and it was *F & P*. While we had been flopping around, becalmed in the rain, Dalts had quietly closed right in on us, having been sailing in good breeze all night.

The Dukes had been up all night on standby and sailing their own watch so when we finally rounded the Horn with light tailwinds they were all too tired to brave the rain to come on deck for a look at what must be one of the most famous landmarks anywhere. Peter read a short service and prayer for Frederick Chapman, scattering his ashes into the sea as we rounded Cape Horn. Watched only by a few albatrosses, we were sure he would have approved. Some of us wondered if we would make our last voyage in a similar fashion one day.

While we were rounding Cape Horn, Jaapi, our shore manager, flew out in an aircraft to uplift video footage by microwave link, which he then rushed back to Punta del Este to be put on satellites for worldwide distribution. The speed at which electronic communication is being developed is mind-boggling and it will not be long before viewers will be able to watch live television footage from the boats as they sail through the Southern Ocean.

Four years earlier on *Lion New Zealand* we had experienced some incredibly rough conditions as we sailed through the Strait de le Maire. This time was to be no different, as we banged and crashed our way through this notorious tidal gate between the Atlantic and Southern oceans. With *F & P* only four miles behind we

We can turn left now, from here every mile north is a mile warmer.

'It's not my fault we're still on the wind ..'

Baz, the ship's philospher, contemplates life, the universe and everything else.

had to keep our foot hard on the pedal. Once through the strait and out into the south Atlantic there were the usual mumblings of 'Bloody Southern Ocean, never going back there again!' Our memories have a terrible habit of being conveniently short, considering we all said much the same thing when on *Lion*.

With 1400 miles to the finish we were clearly going to have our hands full keeping Fishpie at bay. Our first night in the Atlantic saw the breeze crump yet again and Dalts pull up to be almost even with us. Mike was in the nav station and called them up on the VHF, telling them 'You guys really piss me off!' This was answered over the airwaves with a chorus of giggles from the *F & P* nav station.

Merit and *Rothmans* took advantage of our slow progress and they pulled 40 miles out of us to close to within 70 miles. The weather fax was working overtime as Peter and Mike tried to decipher the conflicting maps coming from Argentina and America. A large high-pressure system was developing off the coast of Argentina, so it appeared we were in for some light airs, with which we felt comfortable as we knew we had the legs on *F & P* in those conditions. With 1000 miles to go we were within 100 metres of Fishpie as we sailed to windward in a slowly building breeze. The race was on again and only the best helmsmen were used as we employed harbour-racing tactics to ensure we maintained our slender advantage. It was imperative to remain in the controlling position; had she broken through it would have been very difficult to regain the lead. Throughout the afternoon we changed headsails regularly to squeeze every boatlength out of Big Red. After a few snappy headsail changes we got the slight edge we were looking for and moved out to a tenuous one-mile lead. Who needs the America's Cup for match-racing when you can have racing like this?

Brad decided at dinner-time that night that we needed a bit of extra pep and draped our huge red New Zealand ensign around the galley and played the national anthem over the stereo. Everyone tended to go quiet at these times, but the spontaneous surge of patriotism obviously had the desired effect and we trimmed the sails like men possessed to increase our lead slowly. The greatest drama took

place the next morning when a thumping explosion emanated from down below. Deano nearly had heart failure when the battery box he was sleeping alongside blew its lid off as some wayward battery gas was ignited by a spark on the battery terminals.

With Punta drawing near, Blakey decided it was time to pull out his secret weapon. Often we were asked how we managed to hold off F & P by such narrow margins at the end of each leg. It was not our superior light-airs performance or tactical ability; in fact it was Blakey's neon-bright ski socks that gave us the winning edge each time. We all came to believe in his lucky socks, as whenever he put them on for the last few days it normally spelled the demise of F & P. Their virtue as a source of good luck far outweighed their smell.

Both Big Red and F & P got the better of the conditions over the last few hundred miles as we managed to escape the clutches of a stationary high-pressure system that was still holding the sloops captive. It was this area of high pressure that was to ultimately prove to be the Finnish crew of Martela's saving grace. On the morning of 26 May the radio message that everyone dreads was transmitted from Martela — 'MAYDAY, MAYDAY, OUR KEEL IS FALLING OFF!'. The radio operator only just managed to get out of the hatch as the boat capsized. As Charles Jourdan and Merit were closest to the upturned maxi they altered course and headed towards the stricken crew. On board Big Red the news was sobering and we all held grave concerns for the crew's safety. We were relieved to hear from Merit that everyone was well and accounted for. What would have happened had the capsize occurred in the Southern Ocean does not bear thinking about. Like Drum before the last Whitbread, they were incredibly lucky not to lose anyone. For the crew of Martela the race was over.

However, the race was still very much on for us as we approached the mouth of the River Plate. Earlier Mike had boldly come on deck and told us we would have no more than 25 knots of wind-speed for the last 100 miles to the finish. Twenty-five knots of boatspeed was more like it, as we blasted downwind in winds of up to 55 knots, which, combined with water only 12 metres deep, kicked up a ferocious seaway. F & P was safely tucked away 12 miles astern, so we were able to ease our foot off the accelerator a little to ensure we finished in one piece. As we closed to within ten miles of Punta, the rain squalls cleared, revealing the Fishpie boys, their spinnaker looming out of the mist. Dalts had taken advantage of our slackening of pace and had pushed on relentlessly to close to within four miles. It was instantly back into full race mode for the last miles to ensure we held them out. We scrambled across the finish-line 21 minutes ahead of them — another close one.

Arriving late in the afternoon to a boisterous Uruguayan welcome, we had no difficulty picking out John Lusk, Robi Quilter and Jaapi amongst the crowd, decked out in their green Steinlager clothes. The tensions between the two Kiwi crews were forgotten as we went across to have a beer with our mates on F & P. We had only just pipped them again for our fourth consecutive win, but most importantly we had doubled our lead on the gnomes of Zurich.

We were relieved when we heard over the radio from Merit *and* Charles Jourdan *that they'd rescued the* Martela *crew.*

Leg Four: Auckland — Punta del Este (6255 miles)

Class	Boat Name	Days	Elapsed Time Hours	Mins	Secs	Finishing Position	Handicap Position	Overall Elapsed After 4 Legs
A	Steinlager 2	22	20	41	53	1	1	1
A	Fisher & Paykel NZ	22	21	3	11	2	2	3
A	Rothmans	23	9	0	11	3	3	4
A	Merit	23	10	30	32	4	4	2
A	Charles Jourdan	23	14	18	5	5	5	5
A	Union Bank of Finland	23	18	12	29	6	6	11
A	Gatorade	24	17	28	29	7	7	8
A	The Card	24	18	12	47	8	8	6
A	NCB Ireland	24	23	31	22	9	11	12
A	Belmont Finland II	25	0	45	54	10	12	13
A	Fortuna Extra Lights	25	1	17	31	11	9	7
A	British Defender	25	1	31	12	12	13	9
A	Fazisi	25	7	1	15	13	14	10
A	Liverpool Enterprise	26	2	56	9	14	15	15
C	Equity & Law II	26	15	34	24	15	10	14
CRUISE	Creightons Naturally	26	16	10	48	16	18	18
D	L'Esprit de Liberte	29	3	25	51	17	16	16
D	Schlussel Von Bremen	29	20	33	28	18	19	19
CRUISE	With Integrity	29	21	14	3	19	21	20
D	Maiden	30	12	6	48	20	20	17
D	La Poste	30	15	21	39	21	17	21
A	Martela O.F				DNF			
D	Rucanor Sport				DNF			

CHAPTER NINE

It Ain't Half Hot, Mum

A feature of the stopover in Punta was an incredibly dirty and dingy bar at the end of the breakwater, which was universally known amongst the crews as the 'sleaze bar'. On our first night in town the *F & P* and *Steinlager* crews adjourned en masse to this bar to continue the party started on board *F & P*. There was no problem cleaning up afterwards as the locals literally fought over empty Steinlager cans; this we could never quite understand, but it certainly made cleaning up the boat easier. At our crew meeting the next morning Baz turned up still wearing the same clothes he'd been wearing when we crossed the finish-line, although they were in a somewhat 'well-worn' state. Obviously, Baz was intent on carrying on the celebration as he pulled the tab off another Steinie for breakfast.

Punta del Este was considerably livelier than it had been during our first stopover as the holiday season was now in full swing. The warm weather enticed people to the beach and on a few occasions, when out for a run, we would almost fall over each other as a scantily clad girl sauntered across our paths. Minuscule G-string bikinis seemed to be *de rigueur* in Punta.

Undoubtedly the highlight of our stopover was the 'Whitbread Olympics' hosted by the Cantegril Country Club. The sports to be contested were tennis doubles, in which BC and Pippa Blake flew the *Steinlager* flag, table tennis which Glen never quite got on top of, a running relay, swimming relay, tug-of-war and the premier event — a drinking race. The *Steinlager* swimming team consisting of Marko, BC, Baz and Trae had the crowd in stitches as they lined up on the starting blocks resplendent in shark fins strapped to their backs, which they had manufactured the previous night. However, it was decided for the final that the fins created far too much drag and in a photo-finish the *F & P* boys edged out our team.

Our three big boys — Ross, Grim and Baz — were our entrants in the tug-of-war competition, the only catch being that three girls also had to be in the team. Robi Quilter, Sally Shoebridge and Pippa Blake were coerced into helping out; unfortunately their slim physiques were outweighed by some of the more substantial girls in the other teams. The pressure was on for the final event of the day — the drinking race. Ross was the anchorman for our team and his size ensured there would be few arguments. Being sponsored by a brewery, a loss in this event would have been the ultimate embarrassment. After much argument and finger-pointing our team scored a split-second victory over Dalts and his boys, but it wasn't enough to prevent *F & P* from winning overall, with our team second. The rest of the fleet must have been becoming heartily sick of seeing the two Kiwi crews out in front yet again.

After a total of two months in Punta our grasp of the Spanish language had not progressed a lot further than 'Mucho cerveza por favor!' — this was simply translated 'Lots of beer please!' We were becoming a little more adventurous when ordering

Whenever conditions permitted someone went up to carry out a rig check. This time it's Spike's turn.

food, although most often it was still a stab in the dark. Jaapi, who thought he was coming to grips with the language, was most perturbed one evening at a restaurant when after ordering a meal he was presented with four squashed whole frogs cooked in a light batter. There was an audible gasp around the table as everyone realised that Jaapi had used his pidgin Spanish to order for them also. Much to their relief, the meals turned out to be a little more conventional. Jaapi's South African heritage wouldn't let him back down and he resolutely picked his way through every scrap of frog flesh.

Midway through our stopover Mike had the yacht club in fits of laughter when he bought a huge cream meringue pie and promptly pushed it into Shoebie's face. It was like a scene out of a Charlie Chaplin movie and Shoebie took it all in good grace, although he was to get his revenge some time later. Less enthused by the whole incident was one of the *Merit* crew who said in his suave Swiss accent, 'Why is it zat you Kiwis are so uncouth?'

Our stay in Punta this time was only two-and-a-half weeks, compared with four-and-a-half weeks the first time, so we had no time to get too bored and we were soon preparing to head back to sea for the fifth time. After saying goodbye to our mates on *F & P* and a few of the other boats, we slipped our mooring-lines and motored out into Maldonado Bay to prepare ourselves for the start. There was a distinct feeling of déjà vu on board as we threw a wreath into the sea in memory of the veterans of the Battle of the River Plate, which had taken place within a few miles of Punta del Este.

Billy gives encouragement while Pippa, Robi and Sally give it their all in the tug-of-war competition.

The starting procedure was exactly the same as the first re-start from Punta, although conditions were considerably different with very light and shifty winds seeing *Rothmans* lead around the first turning mark. After a conservative start to ensure we kept our nose clean, we slowly picked up boats to be in third place as we left the Punta skyline behind.

The lead changed regularly throughout the first afternoon as the breeze continued to play cat-and-mouse with us. Shortly after dusk the heavens opened and we sat there going round in circles, trying to keep the boat moving as the wind completely died away. The only visual reference we had were the navigation lights of the other boats, and trying to keep track of them totally confused the helmsman. Dinner on the first night was spaghetti bolognese with real mince, quite a treat on board *Steinlager 2*, before we started on our freeze-dried menu. After the thunderstorms and torrential rain of that first night we were more than happy when dawn produced clear skies and moderate tailwinds. Making a guest appearance amongst the regular four leading boats was *The Card*, clearly benefiting from having a mizzen mast again. By standing out to sea they had jumped to a seven-mile lead.

'Which way to the beach, man?'

At our pre-race briefing Mike told us to expect variable winds for the first few days as we sailed northwards along the Brazilian coast towards Rio de Janeiro, after which we should be into settled tradewind conditions. Mike's predictions had turned out to be wrong, but no-one was complaining as we reeled off the miles in fresh southeasterly winds. With our big red mizzen spinnaker set, we slowly edged away from the opposition and by day three *F & P* and *The Card* were 11 miles astern while *Merit* was 20 miles astern with *Rothmans* a further ten miles back.

The atmosphere on board was altogether different from when we left Punta five months earlier on the second leg down into the 'Big Chilli Bin'. This time we had the more pleasant prospect of warm, tropical tradewind sailing. Gone were the days of taking 20 minutes to get dressed before going on watch; the prospect of rolling out of your bunk and up on deck wearing only a pair of shorts and a T-shirt held significantly more appeal. Little did we know it at the time, but this leg was to prove to be every bit as mentally demanding as the earlier legs, as we coaxed the boat along in very light winds and scorching heat.

By our fourth day at sea, just as we thought we were in for a fast leg, 'Huey' cut off our wind supply 200 miles off the coast of Rio and we found ourselves on the wind in very light, fickle air. Assuming that our competition were suffering from the same fate we switched into light-airs mode, keeping movement around the boat to a minimum as we struggled for every mile. Evidently Lawrie Smith and his boys

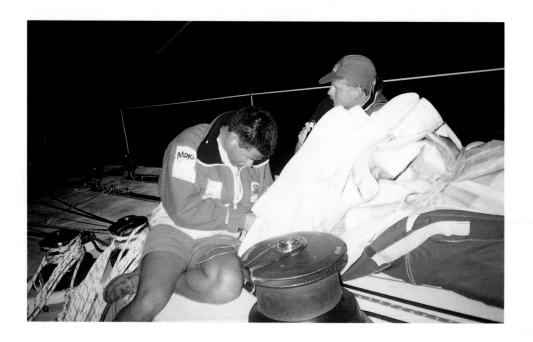

Deano and Goddy spend a night-watch repairing a headsail on the side deck.

on *Rothmans* had decided in Punta that as long as they followed us everywhere they would never make up their deficit of over 50 hours. With this in mind, the *Rothmans* navigator Vincent Geake decided on a course well to the east of the rhumbline in an effort to pick up better breeze than the maps indicated inshore.

Mike and Blakey decided to stay on our current middle-of-the-road course in an effort to keep tabs on our more immediate rivals, *Merit* and *F & P*. The circuitous route taken by *Rothmans* paid big dividends as she picked up the breeze her crew were looking for and over a period of 48 hours she reversed the roles and went from 81 miles behind us to a 25-mile lead. We had committed ourselves to covering the other two boats, so we just had to bite the bullet and watch *Rothmans* continue to march away from us across the chart as over the next few days she extended her lead to 80 miles. While it was frustrating, we were not unduly concerned about *Rothmans* as with 50 hours up our sleeve it was going to take a lot more than an 80-mile lead to have us panicking. The doldrums had yet to be negotiated and we could pick her lead up in one day if she got stuck there.

A source of far greater concern on board, however, was the fact that no-one had remembered to put any sea-water shampoo or soap on board in Punta. In the freezing Southern Ocean you soon learn to live without washing, but in the steamy tropics it's important to wash occasionally to get rid of a few days' build-up of perspiration. BC was becoming a little concerned at the rate with which his

Bucket baths on Copacabana Beach were the order of the day in the tropics.

dishwashing detergent was being used. As he washed the dishes himself every day, he soon figured out it wasn't anyone trying to help out in the galley by doing a few dishes that was reducing his supplies so drastically. All it took was one visit to the aft deck to find the missing detergent, as we began to use it as hair shampoo and soap during our bucket baths. After a few weeks of this treatment there was little fear of any of us being auditioned for a shampoo advertisement. We may not have smelt very good, but at least we were squeaky clean.

Big Red excelled herself in these light on-the-wind conditions. On paper, *Merit* should have eaten us for dinner, but in practice the opposite proved to be the case as we quietly slipped away from the Swiss. The sloop crews, we were to find out later, were becoming more and more frustrated as whenever they thought, 'Here we go — we're into sloop conditions now, the ketches won't be enjoying this!' it turned out that Big Red and *F & P* had enjoyed it after all and had continued to stretch their legs.

Day nine was probably the quietest birthday BC has ever had, although Trae tried to liven up the day by creating an 'alternative' birthday card, made up from some cuttings from the steamier magazines on board that we only ever read for the good stories contained within them. It was one birthday card that was unlikely ever to make it onto the mantelpiece at home. In honour of BC's birthday, 'Huey' rid us of the light headwinds that had been frustrating our progress to the north, and replaced them with 12-knot easterlies as we sailed along the Brazilian coast with the city of Recife in view.

With five sails set we were making good progress as we followed the continental shelf northwards and encountered numerous Brazilian fishing-boats off the coast. Any self-respecting New Zealand fisherman would have cringed with horror at the state of these little boats. It's unlikely any of them would have lasted more than a few minutes in a Cook Strait gale. As we sailed closeby to leeward there were a few twitching nostrils on board Big Red as the stench emanating from those boats was atrocious. Obviously hygiene was of little concern to these fishermen.

We were all starting to feel the heat and the sunblock cream was a valuable commodity as we tried to prevent ourselves from getting too sunburnt. Baz had decided that the sunscreen wasn't doing the job and figured that perhaps the plastic bottle it came in was of more use. With this in mind, he employed some of his boat-building skills and fashioned a 'nose cone' out of the bottle. Once fastened to the bridge-piece of his sunglasses Baz bore a striking resemblance to Robocop and was the brunt of much humour for a couple of days. He was not the only one to wear strange attire; long-sleeved, white, cotton business shirts were popular for avoiding sunburn and anyone watching us sail by could be forgiven for thinking Big Red was being sailed by the Matamata Bowling Club, judging by the number and style of the white sun-hats.

Reaching around the northeast corner of Brazil, we spent a few days where the

With no oven on board, BC cooked everything in pressure cookers.

Dr Mungbean in action during a headsail change.

'What are you going to do after the race?'

wind was so steady we rarely had to change any sails. It was normally feast or famine in this respect, we were either run off our feet in a sail-changing frenzy or we spent long periods without any changes. In these steady conditions we soon became bored and looked forward to any sail changes to break the monotony. In strict accordance with Murphy's law, sail changes were normally called during the standby watch's meal-time, which Goddy observed was akin to going for a quick three-kilometre run between the main course and dessert during an evening meal at home.

During these periods of little action much time was spent telling yet more stories from previous yacht races and trips overseas. It's often amusing to hear how much the same story can be exaggerated over a period of months. No matter how many times you hear the same story, it's still funny. Without doubt the most common topic of discussion on this leg was, 'What will you do after the race?' The scary part was that very few of us actually had anything concrete to carry on with. The general consensus was that most of us wanted to continue sailing full-time, whether it be the America's Cup campaign or racing on the international circuit. To any outsider listening, the topics of conversation may have seemed somewhat monotonous, but the reality of it was that we were in an 84-foot cocoon insulated from current affairs and any other outside news. Upon arrival in Fremantle at the conclusion of the second leg, we had been stunned to hear that the Berlin Wall had come down. We really did live in our own little world that revolved around constantly trying to make that same little world go just that little bit faster in an effort to reach the finish first.

On our eleventh day at sea we were approaching the potentially hazardous

doldrums. The weather maps and satellite photographs were constantly monitored for any clues as to the position and magnitude of the doldrums. It is a natural phenomenon that this unpredictable windless area is narrower on the Brazilian side of the Atlantic than the African. Therefore, the likelihood of being caught out badly was a little less than the risk presented on the first leg when we were further out into the middle of the Atlantic.

As we closed in on the doldrums a 'window' appeared in the towering cumulonimbus clouds on the weather satellite receiver and a course was set to ensure that we took full advantage of this escape route through the potential parking lot. It transpired that we had a remarkably fast transit through the doldrums, hindered only by one night of heavy rain squalls. This period proved to be the undoing of *Rothmans*, as with her position further out to the east she was suffering from a lack of breeze, while *Merit* and *F & P*, close in to the Brazilian coast, had the best of the conditions and had slipped through into the lead. Lawrie and his team on *Rothmans* must have been furious they had taken a gamble and had done well to consolidate it into a good lead, only to have it snatched away by a quirk of the weather. With *Rothmans* now six miles astern of Big Red, and Fishpie in tandem with *Merit* taking up the running 26 miles ahead of us, the race had re-started once more.

Once clear of the doldrums we encountered the northeast tradewinds which were to stay with us right through the Caribbean islands. With the wind from behind us, the ketches rapidly asserted their dominance and bid 'adios' to the sloops as we

Tropical sunset.

set our large mizzen staysails and enjoyed the ride.

Dr Mungbean swung into action the following day when Spike suffered rope burns to his hand during a spinnaker peel and Deano cut his foot while scrambling barefooted around the deck. It was like a scene from 'General Hospital' as he had his patients strewn across bunks; all that was missing were the glamorous nurses. It was quite possibly the biggest disappointment of Trae's life when he discovered that Deano's cut was not serious enough to require any stitches. We had a distinctly uneasy feeling whenever Trae followed us around, as there was growing concern that he might try and cause a few accidents so he could put his training into practice.

As we reeled off the miles towards Fort Lauderdale, life didn't seem too bad at all as we sat in the brilliant sunshine trimming the spinnaker or grinding the sheet. Surrounded as we were by a magnificent deep-blue sea, the Southern Ocean seemed like a very distant memory.

Our progress northeastwards towards the Caribbean was helped by a strong favourable surface current. Sailing past the mouth of the Amazon River, albeit 200 miles out to sea, we experienced some peculiar waves similar to a river in flood. It took the 'brains trust' some time to figure out that the cause of these 'rivers' was a deeper-flowing counter-current, which periodically surfaced and hindered our progress. However, it was not these currents that were the greatest hazard, but rather the return of the dreaded flying fish. It became apparent to us that the word must have spread amongst the flying fish community after our first leg encounters with

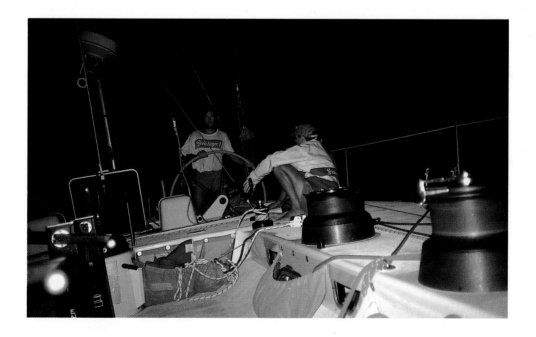

It's certainly no 9 – 5 job . . .

On mornings like this, the Southern Ocean seemed like a very distant memory.

them that we were an easy target. It was no time at all before the all-too-familiar 'Aarghh!' could be heard on deck as these slimy projectiles took apparent delight in bombarding the crew. On many occasions, dawn would reveal a veritable fish market in the bottom of the cockpit consisting of those that had misjudged their trajectory.

The heat was unrelenting as we continued our battle for the lead with *F & P*. As we were sailing downwind there was little air making its way down below decks, with the result that the off-watch lay in their bunks attempting to sleep, panting like fish out of water. On occasions like this we would have given anything for a glass of ice-cold Steinlager. The image of a tall glass with drops of moisture running down the outside of it was almost enough to send anyone insane had they dwelled on it too long. With this in mind, it is not hard to imagine how little sympathy we felt for the Italian crew of *Gatorade* (ex *NZI Enterprise*) when we heard on the inter-yacht sched that their ice-cream maker had broken down.

In an effort to get some elusive sleep, Goddy took a sleeping pill one hot afternoon when coming off watch to help him make the journey to the land of *ZZZZ*. The sleeping pill had the desired effect, but unfortunately for Goddy it had worked too well. Upon waking he discovered that his forehead had a proliferation of graffiti written across it. In the absence of a wall to write on, Goddy's forehead had seemed the next best thing.

As the steady conditions continued, the boredom factor was increasing when someone wrote in the log, 'Goddy steering, Baz trimming, Jaws sleeping — all is normal'. Throughout this leg, filling in the hourly log became a popular pastime. The intensity and length of each log entry was directly proportional to how boring life was on deck. Towards the end of the leg the character assassinations were bordering on being vicious to the point where Blakey called a halt to proceedings until the situation calmed down. No hard feelings were ever intended by any of the literary gems that appeared and it was primarily a way of releasing the pressure valve. It was important that you could take as good as you gave, as tomorrow it might be you on the receiving end of the crew's collective humour. Having an all-Kiwi crew had definite advantages as we all understood each other's culture and knew exactly how far we could go before genuinely offending anyone.

With 1000 miles to Fort Lauderdale we were sailing around the eastern side of the Caribbean islands. It was shaping up for yet another match-race finish with our arch-rivals on the 'white shark', while the sloops were having a very unhappy time further back. Getting stuck in an extended calm patch giving them light tailwinds, the two cigarette boats were suffering severely. As Big Red and *F & P* held the breeze we put a whopping 156 miles on *Merit* in one 24-hour period. 'Marty' Fehlmann and his Swiss crew must have been hating life; they were now back to 268 miles astern, whilst *Rothmans* had not been caught out quite as badly to be 111 miles behind. It was not too difficult to detect an air of bitter frustration in Fehlmann's voice during the position scheds.

Not a lot changed on board Big Red as life continued. The most popular off-watch and standby activity was reading novels. In keeping with our stringent weight-saving policy, we were only allowed to bring one book each. Therefore, it was in your best interests to make sure you brought along a good book, as once read it provided plenty of bartering power when book-swapping negotiations were conducted. Tom Clancy's novels were the best investment, although the library ranged from Ross's and Blakey's Stephen King thrillers to some of the crew's — who shall remain anonymous — Jilly Cooper novels.

The next most popular off-watch pastime was listening to Sony walkmans. Spike and Marko were the leading exponents in this field and could always be found plugged into their walkmans, normally at maximum volume. Goddy held grave fears for Marko's mental stability when he was bopping his way around the inside of the boat jiving to one of his head-banging tapes. Allegedly in the interests of Marko's well-being, Goddy started a petition to have him committed upon arrival in Florida, claiming that it was best for Marko and the rest of the crew's sanity. After a limited response the petition was soon dropped.

Because there is little of outside interest to talk about on board, a big deal is often made of incidents that to an outsider would seem totally trivial. When the early morning light revealed a Milo drink stain liberally splattered across the white radar

The Blues Brothers — BC, Jaws and Goddy — enjoy life on the weather rail.

scanner on the mizzen mast, a kangaroo court was convened immediately to find out who was guilty of this heinous crime. The finger was pointed at Grim and he was rapidly handed down the 'guilty' verdict. The fact that he had not been drinking Milo that night had nothing to do with it — that would have spoilt everyone's fun.

With the finish and our appointment with several cold Steinies looming, the tension stepped up a level on Big Red as we worked our tails off in an attempt to keep the 'white shark' at bay. It was time for Blakey's lucky neon socks to make their presence felt. The inter-yacht scheds were once more being awaited with the apprehension of a parent whose child is undergoing major surgery. If we had held the advantage or put a mile or two on Dalts, someone would dash on deck all smiles with the latest positions. Conversely, if we'd had a bad day losing distance to our compatriots, the news took a little longer to reach the on-watch and was delivered with considerably less enthusiasm.

As the nervous tension built, the biggest arguments on board Big Red began to occur. These concerned the existence of a phenomenon known as 'the green flash'. This is a tiny green flash that is seen just as the last fraction of the sun disappears

Waiting for the green flash.

below the horizon. 'The green flash' only occurs periodically, when the atmospheric conditions and the horizon are perfect. Whilst there were a couple of converts amongst the crew, there were still a few non-believers, the leading figures being Brad and Ross, who claimed those of us who had witnessed this spectacle were hallucinating. The believers, feeling they were God's chosen ones, firmly felt the non-believers were eligible to join the Flat Earth Society.

With a little over 200 miles to the finish, we lay becalmed throughout the night off the coast of Eleuthera, one of the Bahama Islands. At nightfall *F & P* had only been just over the horizon behind us, and we had an anxious night as we constantly monitored the 'stealth' radar for any sign of her in case she slipped around the seaward side of us. We had difficulty keeping track of what was going on as the radar screen was jammed full of huge cruise ships passing us on their way to the Caribbean. It surprised most of us that there were that many cruise ships in the world, let alone just in this corner of the Caribbean.

A few minutes of panic ensued at dawn when we spotted a ketch in front of us on the horizon. As we sat there cursing and swearing, a closer look through the

'Now that's what I call a hamburger!' It could only happen in America.

binoculars revealed that it was a large cruising ketch. A degree of normality returned when Deano went up the rig and spotted *F & P* barely visible on the horizon still behind. At that moment we felt unbeatable, as deep down we always knew that we would come up trumps. This may sound a little arrogant but when push came to shove at the end of each leg we always knew we could do it. Nothing breeds success like success.

The last 200 miles sailing through Providence Channel separating the Bahama Islands was a pleasure as we slid downwind with our mizzen spinnaker set, gybing periodically to take advantage of the windshifts. *F & P* carried a freshening breeze to close to within seven miles as night fell. The notorious Gulf Stream had yet to be negotiated, so we still had a race on our hands. *F & P's* American crewman John Jourdane was something of an authority in this part of town and warranted keeping a close eye on. Sailing across the stream was the highlight of the leg as we pushed Big Red's accelerator hard down with every inch of sail area possible set as the wind increased to 30 knots, giving us a very fast ride down the steep seas through driving rain.

'Welcome to America, Spike.'

Mike called the layline perfectly in the nav station and we found ourselves right on target for the finish-line off Port Everglades. We experienced a moment of panic when we overheard the finishing-boat saying on the VHF radio that they had both yachts on radar three miles from the finish. We nearly had heart failure as five heads collided in front of the radar screen in disbelief. Brad had been constantly monitoring the radar and said, 'No way guys, there is no way they could have caught us.' He was right, as at 4.30 am we surfed across the finish-line under spinnaker at 15 knots. The torrential rain could not dampen our spirits as we heard that *F & P* was, in fact, eight miles behind. After a tense last few days we were very happy Kiwis as we tied up at the magnificent Pier 66 complex, welcomed by many of our wives. With five down and one to go we were tantalisingly close to realising our ultimate dream. A local yachtie watching the celebrations on board said it all as he told us, 'Hey, you guys are really kicking ass and taking names.' We were definitely in America.

Leg Five: Punta del Este — Fort Lauderdale (5475 miles)

Class	Boat Name		Elapsed Time			Finishing Position	Handicap Position	Overall Elapsed After 5 Legs
		Days	Hours	Mins	Secs			
A	Steinlager 2	22	16	41	11	1	1	1
A	Fisher & Paykel NZ	22	17	15	41	2	2	2
A	Rothmans	22	21	33	4	3	3	4
A	Merit	23	10	52	24	4	4	3
A	The Card	23	15	24	19	5	5	5
A	British Defender	23	18	49	47	6	6	8
A	Union Bank of Finland	24	0	33	43	7	7	10
A	NCB Ireland	24	3	24	54	8	9	12
A	Belmont Finland II	24	4	23	0	9	12	13
A	Gatorade	24	5	3	34	10	13	9
A	Fortuna Extra Lights	24	10	7	15	11	14	7
A	Charles Jourdan	24	11	34	24	12	15	6
A	Fazisi	25	1	57	37	13	17	11
C	Equity & Law II	25	20	45	39	14	11	14
CRUISE	Creightons Naturally	25	21	22	18	15	20	18
A	Liverpool Enterprise	26	1	36	30	16	19	15
D	L'Esprit de Liberte	27	2	41	10	17	8	16
D	Rucanor Sport	27	6	14	10	18	10	DNF LEG 4
CRUISE	With Integrity	28	1	17	10	19	22	20
D	Schlussel Von Bremen	28	2	43	3	20	18	19
D	Maiden	28	3	35	18	21	16	17
D	La Poste	30	20	57	38	22	21	21
A	Martela O.F.				DNS			

The Beat Goes On

Rothmans and *Merit* were given a reprieve and experienced fresh tailwinds for the last 150 miles of the leg from Punta, which enabled them to close the gap on the ketches considerably. *Rothmans* arrived in Fort Lauderdale five hours behind us in time for breakfast pancakes, while *Merit* eventually finished 18 hours astern of us. This was exactly what Dalts and his crew had been hoping for as it enabled them to leapfrog into second overall.

The impressive Pier 66 marina complex, where most of the fleet moored, was like an oasis in the desert to us at the end of the hottest and the most tedious leg of the race. The locals could be excused for wondering if the whole event was the Whitbread race or the Steinlager race as New Zealand Breweries USA marketing manager, Jim Robertson, had ensured that everyone in Fort Lauderdale had heard of Steinlager.

Some high-powered lobbying by New York and Annapolis to host the American stopover in the next Whitbread ensured that our Floridian hosts bent over backwards to give us a good time in an effort to retain their stopover status. Throughout our stay there were parties or drinks at a bar in town every night. Our hosts seemed intent on helping us make up for the fact that we sailed 'dry' while at sea. Even the hardiest party animals were unable to keep up with the torrid pace.

Our accommodation was in the form of self-contained apartments complete with a swimming pool on the edge of one of Fort Lauderdale's numerous man-made canals. Sharing the apartments were the *F & P* crew, whom we often socialised with. Any pre-race friction between our two crews had dissipated months ago and we were back to being good mates on shore again, although once at sea it was still a very different story. The adage 'The show ain't over till the fat lady sings' was ringing in our ears and we were well aware that we still had one more leg of 3800 miles to the finish in Southampton before we could sit back and relax.

With this in mind, no stone was left unturned to ensure that Big Red was in a perfect state of readiness for the final leg. We moved the boat to the huge Derektor Gunnell boatyard in Fort Lauderdale to have the rigs pulled out and checked once more. Ross, Grim and Jaws — sometimes referred to as the 'Teenage Mutant Ninja Riggers' — spent hours going over the spars with a fine-tooth comb looking for the slightest possible defect that could result in a broken rig. Meanwhile, Big Red was lifted out of the water and given a new paint job on the keel. Absolutely nothing was left to chance.

Ten days before the re-start, Blakey was quietly going over the whole boat checking it for himself when he spotted a hairline crack in one of the titanium chainplates which hold the main mast up. Immediately Baz swung into action and removed both port and starboard chainplates while Blakey arranged for new ones

Nearly there and the anticipation becomes electric.

to be fabricated at Southern Spars back in Auckland. We tried to keep our problem quiet, although tongues were soon wagging around the boatyard when Baz removed the suspect fittings from the deck.

Once the boat was back into racing trim we all took advantage of a few days' break to have a look around Florida. The road outside our apartments looked more like a starting grid as we rented big Chrysler convertible sports cars and sped off down to the Florida Keys, Disney World and the awe-inspiring Cape Canaveral, where some of us witnessed a spectacular launching of the Space Shuttle.

One of the highlights of the stopover was a performance by the Travelling Boatniks. They were a band made up of guys off the Finnish boats with our own Dr Mungbean on lead vocals. John Osborne, a Kiwi sailing on board *Belmont Finland*, wrote an original song, 'Southern Ocean Blues', which the band performed to an ecstatic crowd at Pier 66.

During the week before the fleet's departure the combined crews of the English boats put together a cricket team to challenge a combined Kiwi team. The Brits were becoming desperate to beat us at something and they figured that a game of jolly old cricket was the perfect way to do it. Unfortunately for their captain Justin Packshaw, off *British Defender,* and his team from old blighty, the *Steinlager/F & P* team also had a few dab hands with a cricket bat amongst them and at the end of the 'One-Day International' we came out on top. Justin couldn't believe they had been beaten by a bunch of colonials.

The final leg had all the makings of being very tricky, with the Gulf Stream to contend with as we sailed up the eastern seaboard of North America before heading eastwards back into iceberg territory and the variable north Atlantic. The day before the start Peter and Mike went up in a helicopter to get a bird's-eye view of the Gulf Stream. This helped to clarify some of the mysteries surrounding the current. At our regular pre-race briefing on the eve of the re-start, Mike outlined our game-plan for the final leg to the finish, explaining that the Gulf Stream is generated by the northeast tradewinds which eddy around the Gulf of Mexico before shooting northwards along the east coast of America, then fanning out eastwards into the Atlantic and dissipating. We discussed the way in which we would sail the boat on this leg — above all else, we had to cross that finish-line in one piece. We would have never forgiven ourselves had we pushed the boat too hard, or done something stupid causing us to lose the rig. However, deep down we all had a burning desire to take out the Grand Slam and finish the race with a perfect record.

It was only fitting that on our last morning in America we indulge in a little American culture and to this end we gave up our crew vans for a convoy of five chauffeur-driven stretched limos for the ten-minute drive down to the boat. Just as we were about to pull out from the dock, Pam, one of the *Maiden* shore crew, rushed past us in search of more wool for spinnaker packing, complaining bitterly, 'The bloody girls knitted it all on the last leg!' We set the tone for the leg by leaving Pier 66 first to head through the 17th Street drawbridge and out into the open sea again. We could hardly hear ourselves think for the noise of throaty V-8 engines. We were surrounded by dozens of huge 'Miami Vice'-type powerboats which are known locally as 'muscle boats'. For the start of this leg we had an extra person on board in the form of Gary Jobson, a well-known American yachtsman and commentator for the cable TV sports network ESPN.

As we milled around before the start relaxing and preparing the boat, Trae made a minor mistake, wrapping a rope around a winch the wrong way. Immediately he was showered with abuse as we called him a 'f.....g two bob' and other assorted good-humoured insults. Gary Jobson couldn't believe his ears and commented that this was 'one tough school'.

In contrast to the well-patrolled start-line in Auckland, the spectator fleet was anchored on a good percentage of the start-line. We hoisted our light spinnaker and big red mizzen staysail and began dodging and weaving our way towards the first turning mark ten miles along the coast. Ironically, it was a huge US Coastguard cutter that was ostensibly controlling the spectator fleet that caused the Whitbread fleet the biggest headaches, as it cut directly across the fleet's path. In particular *F & P* was badly affected by the wayward cutter and Dalts on the helm had to make some drastic course alterations to avoid a collision.

The boat that was undoubtedly attracting most interest from the spectator fleet was *Fazisi*. Throughout their stay in Fort Lauderdale the Russian crew were constantly being gawked at by curious Americans who had never seen a real live Russian before and on many occasions a local could be heard proclaiming, 'Hey, they look just like us.' It seemed to come as a surprise to some of the locals that Russians don't all look like they come from an evil empire and wear Darth Vader masks.

Once clear of the bulk of the spectator fleet we located the first turning mark and gybed towards it. *The Card* had got the best of the start and led us around the mark by one boatlength, with *F & P* and *Merit* engaged in their own private duel 200 metres further astern. On this occasion, Lawrie Smith hadn't been able to make use of his Olympic experience and *Rothmans* had started prematurely, losing valuable time as she re-started. This proved to be a trivial hold-up compared to the problems that lay ahead.

We soon overtook *The Card*, and Gary Jobson took his leave and jumped over the side, almost being run over by the canary yellow ketch in the process as he bobbed about in the water waiting to be picked up by a nearby speedboat. The adrenalin and tension that is always prevalent at a start soon subsided as we settled into our familiar watch-routine and began to concentrate on our objective for the next 18 days — preserving our 35-hour lead over *F & P*. As we sailed downwind that first night at sea we reflected that this project we had all put so much effort into was only a couple of weeks from being over. We were all looking forward to finishing, but we were also a little sad that a great project was coming to an end.

By day two we had no time to dwell on these sentiments as the breeze abruptly swung through to the northwest to put us on the wind. A combination of fresh headwinds and the Gulf Stream running against it at up to four knots resulted in a very nasty seaway. After the cake-ride of leg five it gave us an abrupt reminder that this was the Whitbread race after all as we crashed our way to windward with a double-reefed mainsail and No. 4 jib set. On that evening's sched *Gatorade* informed the fleet they had a problem with their rig after a port spreader broke, necessitating a deviation to St Augustine to effect repairs.

The next day it was the turn of *Rothmans* to head back to port for repairs as the rough conditions persisted. A length of their rod rigging, which holds the mast in column, had broken on an end-fitting and Smith's crew had only just averted a dismasting. Glen wasn't too concerned as it meant his $US100 bet with the *Rothmans* navigator, Vincent Geake, on the outcome of this leg, was looking considerably safer. As *Rothmans* headed for Georgetown to replace the broken rod, the shore crew had two Lear jets flying across America to bring together the people and gear required to ensure a quick turnaround. However, the crew did have time to scoff a quick Big Mac during their impromptu stopover. By the time *Rothmans* put back to sea they had lost a depressing 280 miles.

With this kind of damage occurring around us, we had a timely reminder that a simple gear failure could result in terminal damage. As soon as the conditions

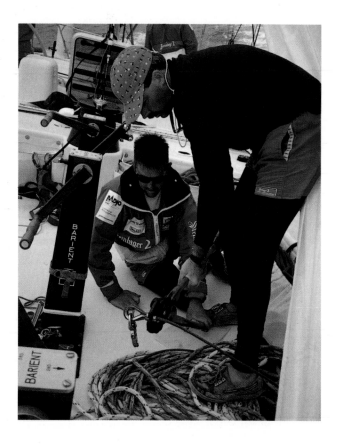

Maintenance continued at sea as Grim and Spike repair a wire halyard.

'Which way do we go?'

moderated slightly, Jaws was hoisted up both rigs to carry out a thorough rig check. Fortunately there were no new cracks in either rig. The only problem was that BC had forgotten to bring aboard any freeze-dried smoked fish for this leg, with the result that our most popular lunch, fish cakes, was off the menu. This was particularly bad news for Blakey as now more of the pasta dishes he loathed were being served instead.

Mike was working long hours in the nav station analysing both the weather and Gulf Stream maps as they poured out of the weather fax. Unpredictable eddies within the stream occasionally caught us out and it was a full-time job trying to keep track of exactly what the warm Gulf Stream was doing. Fishpie was on a more northerly course while we continued to play the middle ground between her and *Merit* out to the southeast. *F & P* played the stream a bit better and stretched out to a 15-mile lead. Perhaps they were benefiting by having Fisher & Paykel managing director, Gary Paykel, along for this leg.

By day four the wind had swung back astern once more and lightened, which together with a sloppy seaway made for some slow progress. With *F & P* away to the north this was no time to get complacent. On this leg there was always the danger that they could make a decisive break by hooking on to a favourable weather system across the north Atlantic and make life very uncomfortable for us. As the wind slowly

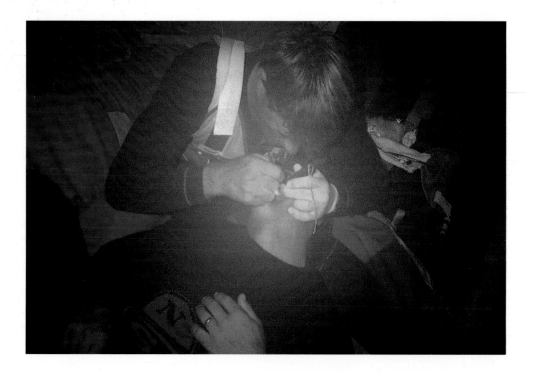

Dr Mungbean putting a temporary filling in Shoebie's mouth. Unfortunately he filled the wrong tooth.

Spike and Baz worked hard to fit a temporary mizzen chainplate at sea.

freshened throughout the day and we wound back up to a more respectable speed once again, we were relieved to hear on the evening sched that we had at least held the 'white shark'. As long as we continued to stay in touch with her a breakage was all that would rob us of overall victory.

It has been said that a person drowning sees their life flash in front of their eyes. For some of us, that was exactly the sensation we experienced as a loud crack shook us out of our reverie. Brad's Kiwi Reds were on deck for the midnight to 0400 watch when at 0150 hours the port mizzen chainplate broke. Initially the titanium fabrication was still holding to the deck, albeit tenuously. Shoebie's watch, on standby at the time, clambered on deck to help drop the big red mizzen spinnaker and the mizzen itself to unload the rig. No sooner had they dropped it than with a sickening 'bang!' the chainplate broke completely.

Only Brad's very fast reaction on the helm saved the rig, as he immediately spun the wheel and threw the boat into a crash gybe in 20 knots of wind. Ross's watch, woken from their deep sleep, raced on deck to find things not as they should be. The mizzen rig was wobbling around like a wet spaghetti noodle as the boat rolled from side to side in response to the swells. Deano climbed hand over hand up the rig to the bottom spreader to tie a length of rope around it and back down to the deck to stabilise the slender spar. Once a few more ropes had been run to further stabilise the rig we were safe again. In addition to coming within a hair's breadth of losing the mizzen we were also in danger of dropping the main mast over the side as the broken chainplate fitting also held the running backstay, which supports the main rig.

The possible consequences of the chainplate failure were too scary to contemplate at the time, although we could not believe we still had a mizzen rig. It was the sort of miracle that we didn't want to question too hard. Perhaps the F & P crew weren't too far from the truth when they claimed God was one of our main sponsors. No-one was to get any sleep for the remainder of the night as everyone remained on deck creating makeshift chainplates out of padeyes bolted through the deck. Once the repair was completed to Baz's satisfaction, the rod rigging was reconnected to the new chainplate and we rehoisted the mizzen to be back up to full speed within six hours.

Throughout the repair we had been forced to sail downwind on the unfavourable starboard gybe and there was a resigned mood amongst the crew that we would have lost a lot of ground to Merit and F & P overnight. Therefore, it was with a degree of pleasant surprise that we spotted Merit only three miles off our starboard beam at dawn. To add cream to the top, the sched position showed that F & P had suffered a slow night also and our position had been preserved. The following day British Defender was not so lucky when her mast toppled over the side as a result of a capstay failing. That really brought home to us how lucky we were to have had such a close shave. Further astern Rothmans was back in the race and she took advantage of strong tailwinds to immediately pull 60 miles out of the leaders.

The journey up through the Gulf Stream was providing plenty of drama for most of the fleet, as we were finding out on the scheds. Tracy Edwards and her crew on *Maiden* banged into a whale, which fortunately resulted in no damage, but were then hit by a 'waterspout' which spun them through a 360° circle, twisting the mast in the process. Since their impressive results in the second and third legs they had been having their fair share of problems. It was impossible not to admire the girls for their gutsy determination in this race. Tracy had her critics, but it was her project and she was to achieve her goal of successfully campaigning an all-woman crew in the Whitbread. *Maiden*'s progress was usually followed with interest on board Big Red as a couple of our crew had formed long-term liaisons with two of Tracy's crew.

A couple of days after our near-dismasting, Blakey decided that he wasn't entirely happy with the structural integrity of our emergency padeyes and together with Baz devised a stronger option. Baz and Spike cut a piece of aluminium engine-bed out and bent it into shape, fabricating a much sturdier chainplate. Once fitted it gave us renewed confidence to push the boat to its maximum once more. Blakey decided to keep our problem quiet until the end of the leg lest it give Dalts or 'Marty' Fehlmann any extra confidence. Peter needn't have worried, as we were to find out later, because *F & P* had also gone close to a second mizzen dismasting when their mizzen forestay had broken.

Ross and Grim packing a spinnaker into a tube bag below decks.

Meanwhile the log-book 'wars' were back in full swing and someone correctly changed the 'comments' heading to 'inane comments'. Shoebie was coming in for all sorts of stick as his watch told him, 'We'll be on deck shortly' and 'I'll make a cup of tea shortly', to which Shoebie retorted, 'Don't call me Shortly!' This particular angle of attack had been started by Baz some months ago on the second leg, and it still managed to get the occasional bite.

Marko hadn't managed to have a haircut in Fort Lauderdale and, deciding he needed to tidy up his act before the finish, asked Spike to cut his hair. BC's bread-mixing bowl was promptly hijacked from the galley and Spike's Hairdressing Salon opened for business on the aft deck. Had he been able to see how his pudding-bowl haircut was turning out, Marko would almost certainly have panicked and called a halt to his 'styling'. The general consensus was that Spike had a limited future as a hairdresser.

By day eight we had sailed out of the warm Gulf Stream and encountered the freezing Labrador Current. There was no doubt we were into the new current as the water temperature plummeted down from a moderate 18° to 1.2° C in less than two hours. Having spent the last three months in tropical climes this abrupt change in temperature came as a bit of a shock. Memories of the Southern Ocean, which had become conveniently distant in our memory banks, came flooding back. The air temperature dropped also and we were once more back into the routine of

wearing several layers of thermal clothing.

The International Ice Patrol reports indicated that our course would take us through an area of 'numerous icebergs and growlers'. Having seen three very large 'bergs Blakey decided to set us a slightly more circuitous course to the south of the heavy ice to reduce the risk of any potential holings as visibility had been greatly diminished in the dense fog around the Newfoundland Banks. Apparently Dalts had no such qualms, and as they had a lot of time to make up to beat us overall, *F & P* continued on the more direct Great Circle course.

Big Red and Fishpie were sharing the lead as the fleet headed eastwards away from the Newfoundland Banks and out into the North Atlantic. The maxis behind were powering up on us as our progress was frustrated by light headwinds. The most noticeable improvement was *Rothmans,* who had really taken the bull by the horns to recover from her earlier setback.

The weather maps indicated that we could expect an extended period of beating to windward. We were stuck behind a slow-moving low-pressure system and until that moved on we were destined to bash our way into the fresh headwinds. We were beginning to wonder if Big Red had only come with a 30,000-mile warranty as numerous shackles and deck fittings began breaking with monotonous regularity. The mainsail and mizzen outhaul shackles broke with suitably spectacular bangs, which was doing nothing for the state of our nerves. After the fright with the mizzen chainplate we just about jumped out of our skins whenever we heard another bang.

We weren't sure how hard to push the boat into the punishing seas as we vied for the lead with *F & P*, which was still over the horizon to the north of us, and the sloops, which were theoretically a lot faster on this point of sail, snapping at our heels. Did we back off to ensure a safe finish and lose ground to the opposition, or push on at full speed and keep our fingers crossed? We ended up with a compromise between the two, by backing off when the sea conditions became lumpy and the boat was slamming, but going flat-out as soon as the seaway allowed it. In this way we managed to keep enough speed on to hold our position and keep in touch with Fishpie.

The wind remained out of the east to keep us on the wind, although occasionally it did ease off. On one such occasion Trae was sitting on the leeward deck trimming the genoa when a school of dolphins started jumping out of the water alongside the boat. Brad went to leeward to have a look and after hearing a few squeaks, Trae asked Brad if he could hear the dolphins talking. Brad claimed he couldn't hear them, while Trae remained adamant he could. The debate continued for a couple of minutes until Brad pulled out of his pocket a toy 'squeaker' that he'd found in a cereal packet that morning, and proceeded to squeeze it in front of an embarrassed Trae. None of us had known that Brad was quite so proficient at dolphin communication.

At dawn on the twelfth day, we finally caught a glimpse of *F & P* for the first time in ten days as we wriggled to windward in very light airs. The previous night Dalts had called us up on the VHF radio to see how we were going. They were

---

Spike's hairdressing salon opens for business on the aft deck.

virtually becalmed under huge black clouds and obviously Dalts was worried that we might do a runner on them. He needn't have worried as we were also going very slowly. Soon after making visual contact with them we split directions in search of a stronger breeze. Unfortunately, it was Fishpie who picked up the fresher breeze and made her escape, moving out to an eight-mile lead.

We were becoming decidedly irritated with the amount of windward sailing we were doing as we tacked on every major shift, resulting in little sleep for the off-watch, who were woken each time and had to shift into a windward bunk. It was even suggested that the song 'And the beat goes on ...' was written for us as we were beginning to feel like the mythical Flying Dutchman, destined to beat to windward for eternity.

It was time for Blakey to put on his lucky fluoro socks once more for the last four days into Southampton. Therefore, it came as no surprise to us the next day when we spotted Fishpie three-and-a-half miles directly to leeward. An air of renewed

Pidgie finds his sea legs.

confidence established itself aboard Big Red as we refocused on holding on to our lead. The sloops weren't coming into us as we thought they would in these conditions, so it was all on with our compatriots once more. With 400 miles still to sail until we reached Land's End on the southwest corner of England, we found ourselves with an unexpected new crew member in the form of a wayward homing pigeon. The bird was on its last legs when it made a crash landing on the deck, but it wasn't long before it was in good health again as we fed it muesli and water.

The pigeon became confident to the point of being cocky and was quite at home wandering around the interior of the boat leaving the kind of deposits everywhere that pigeons are notorious for. On one occasion the bird, which we nicknamed 'Pidgie', was in mortal danger when Bill found one of its offerings on his bunk. Blakey felt sorry for the bird and made up a bed in one of the empty wire pantry-baskets. Pidgie didn't appear to be in any hurry to depart and provided us with a source of entertainment as we carried on with the serious business of repelling the 'white shark'.

With two days still to sail to reach the finish our regular supplies of food ran out. BC pulled out the emergency rations of freeze-dried mince and potatoes, which we ate for breakfast, lunch and dinner. There were a few glances at each other as we tucked into it for the first time and unanimously agreed that it was pretty tasty. Better, in fact, than our so-called 'good' food.

Some of the crew were going loopy as bouts of 'Channel Fever' became rampant on board Big Red as we sighted first the Scilly Isles and then Land's End. This is a strange affliction which turns grown men into babbling idiots when land is sighted at the end of a long ocean race. F & P was still three miles astern and the finish was only 200 miles away. 'Huey' was clearly intent on making us fight the whole way as the breeze disappeared, leaving us becalmed off Lizard Point. F & P closed to within three boatlengths of us as we shouted good-natured abuse at each other. The gentlest of breezes filled in and it wasn't long before we used our light-air speed advantage to wriggle back into a comfortable lead of three miles.

Once more the wind swung around ahead of us and freshened to have us beating to windward along the south coast of England. Fishpie had always enjoyed a slight edge over us in these conditions, so we were sailing like men possessed to maintain our lead. Several helicopters and light aircraft flew out on that penultimate day to witness yet another all-Kiwi match-race for the lead. Evidently Big Red was enjoying the media attention and dug her toes in to keep F & P three miles back. Merit had closed to within 20 miles of us but time was rapidly running out for the Swiss crew.

Throughout our last night at sea we had everyone sitting with their legs over the side to get every ounce of speed out of Big Red. It was working and the F & P boys could make no impact on us. The southern coast of England is notorious for its tidal gates around the main headlands which can literally stop a yacht in its tracks. After a brief park-up off Portland Bill we picked up a new southwesterly sea breeze, enabling us to set all the reaching sails and scoot across Poole Bay to the Needles.

Fishpie had dropped even further astern and with the tide about to turn in our favour for the last 20 miles we slowly began to relax in the knowledge that they couldn't catch us. With numerous spectator boats coming out to meet us, Pidgie decided it was all becoming a bit hectic and flew off towards the shore. One of the first boats out to see us was a press boat with an incredibly excited Peter Montgomery on board. Monty was getting so worked up we were expecting to see him go into orbit any second.

But it was our supporters' boat with our wives, girlfriends and families that we all wanted to see. As we approached the Needles they appeared, jammed into a launch looking like a Vietnamese refugee boat. For our wives and girlfriends it was also the end of a long nine-month race. Many of them had given up their jobs to fly around the world to meet us at the various ports throughout the race. While we were having all the fun and glory they'd been holding down part-time jobs, mowing the lawns and paying the bills. As we set our light spinnaker and red mizzen spinnaker to a roar of approval from our support boat it slowly began to sink in that we were

Big Red glides past the Needles at the entrance to the Solent.

going to do it! This very long race was going to be our own.

There was an incredible atmosphere on board as we completed gybe after perfect gybe down the Solent. Big Red was in her element, showing off to the world's press and we were thoroughly enjoying each other's company together at sea for the last time. Blakey took the helm for the last hour to guide the boat through the hundreds of spectator craft, while the rest of us trimmed the sails and coaxed Big Red along in the dying breeze. Mike was standing on the aft deck, eyes squinted into the late-afternoon sun looking for the fairway marks to make sure we didn't suffer the ignominy of running aground up the tidal Southampton Water.

The anticipation became almost unbearable as we drifted towards the finish-line only one mile ahead until an elusive puff of breeze filled our light spinnaker and whisked us over the line to the boom of a large cannon. As we threw our arms into the air in triumph, emotion took over as we shouted at the tops of our voices. No-one could take that moment away from us. We had given it our all for the past two years and now it was ours.

Entering Ocean Village, to a cacophony of fireworks, we were stunned at the crowds lining the marina to welcome us. Our faces were set in permanent ear-to-ear grins as hundreds of Kiwis, many of whom had been waiting for three days,

'It was our supporters' boat with our wives, girlfriends and families that we all wanted to see.'

The Kiwi flag flies proudly as after 33,000 miles it's ours.

cheered us into the dock. Whitbread race committee chairman, Charles Williams, presented Blakey with our sixth Beefeater Trophy and, more importantly, the magnificent Whitbread Trophy.

As the champagne corks flew and our wives and families clambered aboard to join the party we stopped to applaud Grant Dalton and the *F & P* crew, who had finished 36 minutes behind us. A simple handshake and a look into their eyes was all that was required. Like us, they had given this race their hearts and souls and had been formidable competitors. We were all proud to have finished the race with an emphatic Kiwi first and second. The fact that this was Dalts's first attempt as a skipper made their result especially creditable.

That evening, as we enjoyed the party being thrown at the Royal Southampton Yacht Club by *Steinlager 2*'s three trustees, many of us slipped out onto the balcony, leaving the noise of the party behind to sneak another look at our magnificent Big Red as she lay motionless alongside the dock awash with floodlights — her job completed at last.

Leg Six: Fort Lauderdale — Southampton (3831 miles)

Class	Boat Name	Days	Elapsed Time Hours	Mins	Secs	Finishing Position	Handicap Position
A	Steinlager 2	17	0	23	15	1	1
A	Fisher & Paykel NZ	17	0	59	40	2	2
A	Merit	17	2	43	45	3	3
A	Rothmans	17	12	50	3	4	5
A	The Card	17	19	7	25	5	7
A	Belmont Finland II	17	20	35	27	6	8
A	Fortuna Extra Lights	17	21	44	56	7	6
A	Fazisi	18	4	21	9	8	9
A	Union Bank of Finland	18	6	8	57	9	10
C	Equity & Law II	18	10	8	48	10	4
A	NCB Ireland	18	13	29	10	11	11
A	Gatorade	18	15	44	49	12	13
A	Charles Jourdan	18	16	1	34	13	12
A	Liverpool Enterprise	19	3	45	24	14	14
CRUISE	Creightons Naturally	19	19	4	50	15	15
D	Schlussel Von Bremen	22	5	35	46	16	18
D	L'Esprit de Liberte	22	5	59	1	17	17
D	Rucanor Sport	22	17	45	56	18	19
D	Maiden	22	17	59	8	19	20
D	La Poste	22	23	40	48	20	16
A	British Defender	23	16	26	24	21	21
CRUISE	With Integrity	24	17	26	10	22	22
A	Martela O.F.				DNS		

The looks on our faces tell it all.

No Buts...

Some of the other competitors complained to the *Steinlager 2* crew that we had spoiled the race for them. They preferred a more swashbuckling adventurous style, staggering down to the boat on the morning of the start still three sheets into the wind after a big rage the previous night. They seemed to object to the fact that the Steinlager Challenge was a smooth, well-oiled machine. It was very noticeable which syndicates were the best organised. It was always *Steinlager, Fisher and Paykel, Merit* and *Rothmans* that were oases of calm amidst the last-minute frenzied rush that usually preceded a leg start. Some commented that we were all clones of each other, and this was true to a certain extent, but it was the only way it could work. There is no place for a boatload of prima donnas in the Whitbread race — they won't last the distance. You had to sell your soul to the company, dress like a Steinlager bottle each day and become a bit of a 'yes' man. But at the end of the race we had won; there had never been a bad word on board; we had kept the same happy crew the whole way around, and made friends amongst the crew that will last a lifetime.

Our relationship with the Fishpie boys matured as the race progressed. Naturally enough feelings between the *Steinlager 2* and *Fisher and Paykel* camps were running high before the race because we both wanted to be the top New Zealand boat. This strained the relationship in the early days somewhat, but gradually it progressed to one of admiration and friendship as we battled it out on the race course. The two crews were fiercely competitive whether it be out on the race track or in any sporting competitions that we enjoyed on land. It didn't matter where you came overall in a swimming race, for instance, so long as you beat the other Kiwi team. Being competitive probably helped us both on the race course as we had to sail at 100 per cent all of the time to beat the 'white shark', whereas some of the other yachts, without an immediate competitor to race against, might have slackened off that half a per cent. Some of the other crews used to wonder if the two Kiwi crews actually liked each other, but in truth this rivalry was confined to the race course, and we were the best of mates in the pub afterwards.

It was at one of the after-match functions at Fort Lauderdale that a couple of *Rothmans* crew members told us that they firmly believed that *Steinlager 2* used to cruise through 90 per cent of each leg and then put the accelerator down for the last stretch to pass *F & P* and take the leg win. Nothing could be further from the truth. We had to give everything to beat *F & P* and there was never anything left in reserve at the end of each leg. It must have been extremely hard for Grant and his boys to put in just as much effort and heartache and yet never quite get the result they so badly wanted.

Before the start of the Whitbread Pierre Fehlmann, when asked about the ketch versus sloop debate, commented that the only advantage in a ketch was that it was

'And the sloops wondered why we passed them on a reach.'

easy to convert into a cruising boat after the race. By the end of the race, both he and Lawrie Smith were leading proponents of the sour grapes brigade, claiming that the ketches had enjoyed an unfair advantage. We were beyond worrying about these statements as the rule had been there for everyone to use. We believe Smith and Fehlmann both investigated the ketch option, but disregarded it for their own reasons — a decision they were later to regret. A senior crew member of *Rothmans* told us after the race that they had investigated the ketch concept, but had shelved the idea as they felt they had run out of time to develop it properly.

Some of the old salts around town will probably say, 'You chaps have got so much fancy computer gear on board that you're superfluous.' It is true that we did have a lot of sophisticated equipment on board to help us, but you still have to get up on deck and sail the boat yourself. You've still got to reef the mainsail, set the spinnaker, and decide whether the big black cloud behind you has much wind under it. The computers won't tell you how to sail the boat, they will only tell you if you are sailing the boat well enough. You won't get anywhere without some form of instrumentation to help you get the best out of your boat. The days of 'seat-of-the-pants' sailing have gone if you want to win the Whitbread.

Big Red in her element.   *Tools of the trade.*

Young yachtsmen often ask how they can get to crew in a Whitbread race. Unfortunately there is no easy answer to that question. Human nature being what it is, you tend to choose people whom you know and trust. This probably applies to any sport or business. You naturally choose people you have sailed with before, guys you know are good helmsmen and trimmers and have the attributes needed to contribute something on such a long campaign as the Whitbread. This does tend to make it a bit of a 'closed shop' when it comes to a youngster trying to get on a boat for the first time. He may be an excellent sailor, the equal of many of the crew, but you just don't know him. However, in the same breath, you do need new blood and youthful enthusiasm on board to keep Dad's Army on their toes. So for those who have their hearts set on competing in a Whitbread, or the 'round the twist' race as it is more affectionately known, one can only suggest that you get as much experience in ocean racing as you can. This applies especially to overseas contests. Sooner or later somebody is going to say, 'Hey, I know this guy who's pretty good, I sailed with him in Hawaii . . .'.

One of the strengths of the *Steinlager* campaign was the leadership. Blakey always led from up front and he pushed himself harder than anyone else on the boat. It's difficult to grumble about the skipper when he's alongside you on the foredeck helping with a headsail change, getting just as wet and cold as you are. He wasn't afraid to spend money, or ditch something that wasn't performing up to expectations. Blakey

Some of the best sailing of your life.

never put anyone above anybody else on the boat and allowed for people to have good days and bad days.

The Whitbread race is such a long race through such extremes in conditions that a lot of the crew seemed to develop a love/hate relationship towards it. You experience some of the worst sailing of your life, but also some of the best. The worst for most of us ranged from the miserably cold conditions of the second leg to the boredom of tradewind sailing along the Brazilian coast in the fifth leg. Morale reached an all-time low on the leg to Fremantle, perhaps because it was much colder than we expected; we had gear breaking left, right and centre, and for the first time in the race we had our tails between our legs as we dropped off the back of the leading bunch. It was a thoroughly miserable time, but one which we can't complain about as we were down there by choice.

In contrast with those dark days we had some wonderful sailing. There's little in this world that can compare with the knee-trembling thrill of surfing an 84-foot maxi down a huge wave at 25 knots, burying her completely underwater at the next wave; the boat then popping out, shaking herself off and roaring off down the next wave, the crew all soaking wet but grinning like Cheshire cats.

You experience things that you would never see in a lifetime of harbour sailing; gliding past the beautiful yet dangerous icebergs with their incredible translucent white luminescence. We spent hours watching the huge albatrosses with the tips of their wings skimming inches from the waves. Or perhaps the aurora australis; we would lie on the deck looking up, seeing the reds and greens of the southern lights shimmering like curtains in the sky.

It is a race of extraordinary mental highs and lows, from the depression of being behind in the Southern Ocean to the ecstasy of winning, that incredible release of tension at the sound of the finishing gun. As Shoebie said, 'You don't realise how much fun it was until it finishes. You just can't wait to finish, and then when you do you look back and say, "Well that's been a bloody good three years".'

The race was over and as the guys one by one left the campaign to fly home they all quietly walked the length of the dock in the Hamble, reached out to the boat for the last time and patted her, saying, 'Thanks Big Red.'

She was a very special boat.

It's ours at last.

1989/90 WHITBREAD ROUND THE WORLD RACE RESULTS
(32,926 miles)

Class	Boat Name	Days	Elapsed Time Hours	Mins	Secs	Finishing Position	Handicap Position	Average Speed In Knots
A	Steinlager 2	128	9	40	30	1	1	10.7
A	Fisher & Paykel NZ	129	21	18	22	2	2	10.58
A	Merit	130	10	10	14	3	3	10.54
A	Rothmans	131	4	54	23	4	4	10.48
A	The Card	135	7	15	43	5	5	10.16
A	Charles Jourdan	136	15	14	51	6	7	10.06
A	Fortuna Extra Lights	137	8	14	11	7	6	10.01
A	Gatorade	138	14	30	12	8	8	9.92
A	Union Bank of Finland	138	16	38	12	9	9	9.91
A	Belmont Finland II	139	4	31	13	10	10	9.88
A	Fazisi	139	9	1	4	11	12	9.86
A	NCB Ireland	139	19	22	38	12	13	9.84
A	British Defender	143	12	42	23	13	14	9.58
C	Equity & Law II	148	23	50	33	14	11	9.23
A	Liverpool Enterprise	151	4	52	22	15	17	9.1
CRUISE	Creightons Naturally	162	6	34	58	16	20	8.47
D	L'Esprit de Liberte	164	21	36	16	17	15	8.34
D	Maiden	167	3	6	53	18	16	8.2
D	Schlussel Von Bremen	167	19	7	34	19	18	8.19
CRUISE	With Integrity	170	16	19	7	20	21	8.05
D	La Poste	181	22	56	17	21	19	7.5
A	Martela O.F.				DNF Leg 4			
D	Rucanor Sport				DNF Leg 4			

1989/90 WHITBREAD ROUND THE WORLD RACE AWARDS

CATEGORY	WINNER
Whitbread Trophy (Division A — 1st on Elapsed Time)	*Steinlager 2*
Division A — 2nd on Elapsed Time	*Fisher & Paykel NZ*
Division A — 3rd on Elapsed Time	*Merit*
Division C — 1st on Elapsed Time	*Equity & Law II*
Division D — 1st on Elapsed Time	*L'Esprit de Liberte*
Division D — 2nd on Elapsed Time	*Maiden*
Division D — 3rd on Elapsed Time	*Schlussel Von Bremen*
IYRU — Best 5 out of 6 legs — 1st	*Steinlager 2*
IYRU — Best 5 out of 6 legs — 2nd	*Fisher & Paykel NZ*
IYRU — Best 5 out of 6 legs — 3rd	*Merit*
Non-Maxis — 1st on Handicap	*Equity & Law II*
Non-Maxis — 2nd on Handicap	*L'Esprit de Liberte*
Non-Maxis — 3rd on Handicap	*Maiden*
Cruiser Class — 1st on Elapsed Time	*Creightons Naturally*
Cruiser Class — 1st on Handicap	*Creightons Naturally*
First on Handicap Overall	*Steinlager 2*
Roaring Forties Trophy (1st on Handicap Legs 2, 3, and 4)	*Steinlager 2*
Best Crew Competing for the First Time	*Maiden*
Greatest Distance Over 24 Hours	*Fortuna Extra Lights*
Excellence in Communications	Peter Blake
Most Outstanding Act of Seamanship	Lawrie Smith
Most Outstanding Skipper	Grant Dalton
Most Distinguished Performance by a Doctor	Claire Russell *(Maiden)*
Best Kept Log	*Charles Jourdan*
Bubbly Personality Award	Justin Packshaw *(British Defender)*

STEINLAGER CHALLENGE SPONSORS

The Steinlager Challenge acknowledges the sponsorship and support of the following companies:

New Zealand Breweries
New Zealand Breweries was the principal sponsor of the Steinlager Challenge and initiated the project in association with Peter Blake.

Epiglass (Gold Sponsor)
The original Gold Sponsor of the Challenge, Epiglass provided the high technology building materials and coatings that were used in the construction of the Steinlager yachts.

Radio New Zealand (Silver Sponsor)
New Zealand's national radio network has more than 50 stations. Their internationally recognised commentator, Peter Montgomery, is the voice of yachting.

Commercial Photographers (Silver Sponsor)
Auckland's leading commercial processing company was responsible for supplying all photographic services to the Challenge.

New Zealand Line (Silver Sponsor)
New Zealand Line organised the shipping of equipment by sea to various Whitbread ports and shipped *Steinlager 2* to England.

EXCLUSIVE SUPPLIERS

Canterbury International
The familiar 'CCC' logo is on the crew's Canterbury clothing. Canterbury manufacture and market the exclusive Steinlager Challenge clothing range.

Canon
Business equipment used in the administration of the Steinlager Challenge was supplied exclusively by Canon.

Dorlon
The excellent wet-weather gear worn by the crew was manufactured and supplied by Dorlon.

Owens Group
A long-time supporter of Peter Blake, Owens Group provided road transportation and lifting facilities for the Steinlager yachts.

Barient
The specialised winch equipment for the yacht was supplied exclusively by Barient.

Kinnears Ropes
The Southern Ocean ropes on *Steinlager 2* were provided exclusively by Kinnears Ropes.

Comworth Systems
Oki mobile telephones were used in the Challenge vehicles and aboard the yacht.

CED Distributors (Apple Computers)
Apple computers were used for administration and became an integral part of *Steinlager 2*'s navigation system.

RIGHTS SPONSORS

Lusty & Blundell
Electronic equipment for the Steinlager yachts was supplied by Lusty & Blundell.

Crystal Electronics
Crystal Electronics co-ordinated and installed the complex electronics package aboard *Steinlager 2*.

Impressions International
The production and application of sponsor decals was by Impressions International.

Invincible Inflatables
The inflatable tender boat for the Steinlager yachts was supplied by Invincible Inflatables.

Black & Decker
Black & Decker supplied the power tools used in the building and maintenance of *Steinlager 2*.

Sony
The Video 8 cameras, cassettes and walkmans used on *Steinlager 2* were supplied by Sony.

DHL
We used DHL's international courier facilities around the world.

Deloitte Haskins & Sells
Deloitte Haskins & Sells were auditors to the Steinlager Challenge.

Vita Sleeping-bags
The best four hours of our day in the Southern Ocean were provided by Vita.

Easypark Ltd
Car parking at the Challenge headquarters was at Easypark.

Willis Faber
Insurance for the Steinlager Challenge was provided by Willis Faber.

11 May 1990
British Defender loses top 40 per cent of her mast with a rigging failure, and carries on to finish under jury rig. *NCB Ireland* also suffers rigging failure and uses the anchor chain to keep the mast up.

22 May 1990
Steinlager 2 completes the grand slam by winning every leg, with total elapsed time of 128 days 9 hours 40 minutes 30 seconds.

7 May 1990
Gatorade breaks a spreader on her mast and returns for repairs. *Rothmans* breaks a stay on her mast and returns to Georgetown for repairs. Weather pattern allows *Rothmans* to catch up 200 miles on the leaders in seven days. *Steinlager 2* suffers near-loss of her rigs when the mizzen chainplate breaks.

LEG 6
3,831 Miles

SOUTH
En

6 September 1989
UBF stops in Madeira for a new headboard car and other rigging repairs.

FORT LAUDERDALE
Florida

8 September 1989
Creightons Naturally stops in Tenerife for repairs to spinnaker pole end fitting.

8 May 1990
Maiden is hit by a waterspout, which spins the boat through 360° and damages her mast.

LEG 5
5,475 Miles

LEG 1
6,281 Miles

5 Septer
One cruc
Finisterre
Steinlage
win. Perk
was won

11 October 1989
Tragedy for the Russians when *Fazisi* skipper, Alexei Grishenko, commits suicide by hanging himself, apparently because of the pressures of being the first Soviet Whitbread skipper.

20 March 1990
Rothmans gambles by taking a more easterly course, and leads the fleet by 80 miles for a week. Her moment of glory is short-lived as the ketches race by in tradewind sailing.

22 September 1989
Fisher & Paykel breaks mizzen mast when weld fails, but manages to stay in third place. *Rothmans* falls heavily off a big wave and splits her deck open.

18 October 1989
L'Esprit de Liberte is nearly stranded when their sponsorship money goes missing.

20 October 1989
Swede Janne Gustafsson, a very popular crewman on *The Card*, is killed in a motorbike accident.

PUNTA DEL ESTE
Uruguay

1 November 1989
Creightons Naturally returns to Punta del Este when a port shroud breaks.

LEG 4
6,255 Miles

CAPE HORN

26 February 1990
Martela capsizes after her keel falls off. Luckily all the crew are rescued by *Merit* and *Charles Jourdan*.

9 November 1989
The Card crew member, Etienne Giroire, breaks his arm after being swept along the deck. On *Fortuna Extra Lights* Rafael Tibua breaks his ankle and Santi Portello dislocates his shoulder in similar fashion.

12 November 1989
Two crewmen are swept overboard from *Creightons Naturally* when she broaches in a storm. Both are recovered but only one survives; Tony Phillips is buried at sea.

1
Je
o
re
w
lu
m
th